Small Business and Practice Management for Paralegals

Rebecca Bromwich

emp 2010
Emond Montgomery Publications
Toronto, Canada

Emond Montgomery Publications Limited
60 Shaftesbury Avenue
Toronto ON M4T 1A3
http://www.emp.ca/highered

Printed in Canada.
Reprinted July 2013.

We acknowledge the financial support of the Government of Canada through the Canada Book Fund for our publishing activities.

Acquisitions and development editor: Peggy Buchan
Marketing manager: Christine Davidson
Director, sales and marketing, higher education: Kevin Smulan
Supervising editor: Jim Lyons
Copy editor: Sarah Gleadow
Production editor: Debbie Gervais
Proofreader: Diane Gula
Indexer: Paula Pike
Cover designer: Tara Wells
Cover image: studiovision/iStockphoto

Library and Archives Canada Cataloguing in Publication

Bromwich, Rebecca
    Small business and practice management for paralegals / Rebecca Bromwich.

Includes index.
ISBN 978-1-55239-356-7

    1. Legal assistants—Ontario.   2. Small business—Management.   3. Practice of law—Ontario.   I. Title.

KEO168.L43B76 2010   340.023'713   C2009-906911-3
KF320.L4B76 2010

For Desmond Bromwich

Contents

Chapter 8   File Management and Time Management

PART I

Operating a Small Business

CHAPTER 1

Introduction and Overview

CHAPTER OBJECTIVES

After completing this chapter, you should be able to:

- Explain what the Law Society of Upper Canada is and understand its role in regulating paralegals.

- Recognize certain traits required to be a successful entrepreneur.

- Understand the factors to consider when deciding whether or not to start your own paralegal business.

ENTREPRENEURSHIP, INNOVATION, AND WORK AS A PARALEGAL

The Law Society of Upper Canada (LSUC) defines a **paralegal** as a person who provides legal services. **Legal services** in turn are defined as "conduct that involves the application of legal principles and legal judgment with regard to the circumstances or objectives of a person" (*Law Society Act*, s. 1(5)). The LSUC's Paralegal Rules of Conduct outline the scope of the services that paralegals are allowed to provide in Ontario, as well as specific rules regarding how they are to provide those services. The LSUC grants licences to individuals who are qualified to work as paralegals and can impose sanctions on those who do not comply with its rules and regulations—for example, by revoking their licences or fining them.

The **Law Society of Upper Canada** is a professional organization that governs legal services in Ontario. Its mandate is to ensure that the people of Ontario are served by lawyers and paralegals who meet set standards of education, competence, and conduct. Founded in 1797 to allow lawyers to govern their colleagues' conduct and protect the public, the LSUC has regulated lawyers for centuries.

In 2007, the LSUC began licensing and regulating paralegals with the aim of providing the people of Ontario with more choice and protection and improved access to justice. The LSUC's decision to do so made Ontario the first province to license paralegals and regulate the profession. Paralegals who practise in Ontario have obligations to their clients, to the general public, and to the administration of

paralegal
an individual who provides legal services and representation in permitted practice areas, and who has a licence to do so issued by the LSUC

legal services
services that involve applying legal principles and legal judgment to the circumstances and objectives of a client

Law Society of Upper Canada (LSUC)
a professional organization that governs legal services in Ontario with a mandate to ensure that the people of Ontario are served by lawyers and paralegals who meet set standards of education, competence, and conduct

justice; prospective licensees must demonstrate to the LSUC that they have experience providing legal services, pass a licence examination, pay fees, and meet other requirements relating to good character and training.

Unlike law clerks, who must work under the supervision of a lawyer, paralegals can operate private practices. Regardless of how proficient a paralegal is with respect to legal matters, the success of his or her practice will depend to a large extent on efficient and effective business management. Effective advertising and marketing, client management, accounting systems, bill collection, insurance, and staff supervision are important factors contributing to success.

Paralegals must always observe the professional obligations imposed on them by the LSUC. In addition to handling matters in the above areas effectively, paralegals preparing to start their own business must be aware of limitations on their conduct and the nature of their work, and must keep their professional knowledge current.

Improper behaviour by legal professionals can have potentially devastating consequences for both clients and the public. Refer to the LSUC's Paralegal Rules of Conduct ("the Rules") and the Paralegal Professional Conduct Guidelines ("the Guidelines"), which can be found in the "Paralegals" section of the Law Society's website (www.lsuc.on.ca).

ENTREPRENEURIAL SELF-ASSESSMENT

entrepreneur
an individual who starts
up a new business

As leaders of small businesses, **entrepreneurs**—those who organize and manage an enterprise, especially a business—are responsible for a high degree of business innovation, often developing new and better ways of doing things. As sole proprietors, they can make decisions and act without the need to convince others of the validity of their ideas or obtain permission beforehand. On the other hand, entrepreneurs assume a high level of personal stress and financial risk. For paralegals, these challenges are amplified by the added responsibilities and obligations of running a small business within a regulated profession, since entrepreneurial initiative must operate within the parameters of the LSUC rules.

Entrepreneurship involves a particular skill set and range of tasks, as well as considerable risk. While estimates vary, more than half of small businesses fail within the first five years. The success or failure of a small business that provides human services, such as legal services, depends in part on the trade skills of the entrepreneur, but business acumen is also significant.

Not everyone is suited to running a small business, and assessing whether or not becoming an entrepreneur would be a good choice for you can be challenging. The following are some personality traits to consider.

Initiative

Things may come to those who wait, but only the things left by those who hustle.

—Abraham Lincoln

Above all others, the trait that is generally acknowledged as the most important for entrepreneurs to possess is a willingness to take initiative and get things moving. As their own bosses, entrepreneurs must be self-starters; no one is watching them to ensure that they perform their work.

Prospective entrepreneurs should enjoy taking on leadership roles and should not need to rely on others to provide them with direction. Motivation, self-discipline, and a positive attitude are important prerequisites for entrepreneurial success. The best entrepreneurs often thrive on challenge.

Interpersonal Skills

To be successful, you have to be able to relate to people; they have to be satisfied with your personality to be able to do business with you and to build a relationship with mutual trust.

—George Ross

The provision of legal services is a particularly people-oriented activity. It is a service industry in which you are selling credibility and trust. The ability to communicate effectively with clients and the public face to face, over the telephone, and in writing is an important skill for legal professionals to possess.

Social boldness—for example, the ability to strike up conversations with new people—is another important quality, as you must be able to network, foster new business relationships, and ultimately convince others to buy your services. You will also require social confidence and negotiation skills when dealing with opposing counsel on behalf of your clients.

The ability to network with colleagues and mentors is also useful. Entrepreneurs who seek out and rely on expert advice from senior colleagues and professionals are much more likely to see their business revenues increase than those who do not. This may also be a source of referrals.

Entrepreneurial paralegals must deal with suppliers, such as document servers and couriers. Larger operations may require staff, and management skills will be important.

Calculated Risk Taking

Often the difference between a successful person and a failure is not one has better abilities or ideas, but the courage that one has to be on one's ideas, to take a calculated risk—and to act.

—André Malraux

When opening their small businesses, entrepreneurs assume many forms of risk—for example, in deciding who to hire, where to locate, where to advertise, and whether or not to take on particular business partners.

People who are risk-averse—those who prefer to "play it safe" and stay within the existing frameworks of their jobs—are probably not ready to take on the responsibility of entrepreneurship. On the other hand, those who are too willing to take risks may act recklessly and endanger their businesses.

The best entrepreneurs are those who assess situations carefully and then determine whether or not particular risks are worth taking, basing their decisions on a reasoned assessment of the possible consequences of different courses of action.

Decisiveness

If I had to sum up in a word what makes a good manager, I'd say decisiveness. You can use the fanciest computers to gather the numbers, but in the end you have to set a timetable and act.

—Lee Iacocca

Entrepreneurs are their own bosses. If you like clear structure and directions before and during a task and constructive feedback upon completing it, you are probably more suited to working as an employee than running your own business. Similarly, if it is difficult for you to decide on a course of action—whether because you tend to act rashly, without considering alternatives, or because you have trouble making up your mind—you may not be suited to being your own boss.

People who make good entrepreneurs are confident, enjoy making considered decisions, and like being in charge. They must be sufficiently decisive to make decisions independently and to deal with the consequences of those decisions sensibly.

Planning and Skills

Good fortune is what happens when opportunity meets planning.

—Thomas Alva Edison

Because they are responsible for planning where their businesses should go in the future, entrepreneurs must be able to make both short- and long-term plans. In order to do so, they must be organized and must take responsibility for seeing tasks through to their conclusions.

Specialized education and/or training can be important to an entrepreneur's success. A 2004 report found that small businesses run by individuals with a post-secondary education experienced more than twice the revenue growth of those run by individuals with less than a high school education over the same period of time (CIBC World Markets Inc. 2004). Taking the time to acquire business knowledge and skills—in addition to professional knowledge and skills particular to paralegals—through continuing education, self-study, and work experience will increase your chances of success.

Flexibility

Stay committed to your decisions but stay flexible in your approach.

—Tom Robbins

Entrepreneurs are commonly viewed as people who are very responsive to change and who have the ability to perceive opportunities that others may not see. Because there is no "boss" to consult or convince beforehand, entrepreneurs are often in a position to make decisions quickly, which can allow them to benefit from new opportunities as they present themselves. For example, a paralegal who sets up a business with the intention of defending traffic tickets for clients may be wise to reconsider if offered a sizable contract to do debt collection work.

While advance planning is crucial for success, equally crucial is your ability to "keep your ear to the ground" without losing sight of overall goals, and a willingness to modify your business plan as circumstances change.

Resourcefulness

At the outset of your career as an entrepreneur, you may be a one-person operation. To reduce your start-up and operating costs, you should consider taking on some basic tasks yourself. This might mean painting your office yourself; setting up your own computer, printer, and fax machine; assembling your own furniture; buying your own office supplies; and so on. You will not have an IT department or secretary to rely on, and may have only yourself.

It is also important to determine what you can do yourself and what requires expert assistance. For example, even if you intend to do your own bookkeeping, it may be wise to consult with an accountant for the initial set-up of your accounting system. Alternatively, your time might be better spent on marketing initiatives than on painting your office, and you might decide to hire a student to do the painting even if you are capable of doing it yourself.

Investment

Sometimes your best investments are the ones you don't make.

—Donald Trump

One of the major reasons why it is risky to be an entrepreneur is that, as the saying goes, "it takes money to make money." Starting a business can be expensive. Entrepreneurs need capital to invest toward office rental, insurance, Internet and phone, advertising, and other office expenses before they can earn any money from their business.

Unfortunately, the payoff from operating a small business is often slow to materialize. Entrepreneurs can probably expect to lose money in the first year—or even the first few years—of operating a business. Cash flow shortages are typical. Nonetheless, taking on excessive debt is often what sinks a business. Planning appropriately for expenditures through credit that can realistically be carried and eventually paid back is a crucial aspect of the planning process (see, for example, Girard 2007).

Some fortunate individuals will have money saved. For others, saving money may be a motivation for working as an employee for a while after graduating. This has at least two benefits: allowing you to save money to invest in your business, and allowing you to gain skills that will make your business a safer investment.

For the majority, who must borrow money, having good credit will help. Checking your credit rating and cleaning up any problems may be essential. A line of credit will supply you with money at a much lower cost than a regular credit card, but it may be difficult to acquire a line of credit without a steady income. If you are employed before you open your own business, you should apply for a line of credit at that time. It may also be necessary to offer security, such as equity in a home. If, like most recent graduates, you do not yet own a home, consider whether you have a relative willing to guarantee your line of credit.

Support Network

A wide support network of family and friends can be instrumental to your success. From such a network you may be able to obtain a financial investment or support from family members, assistance with the start-up process from friends with particular expertise, and/or advice from mentors and colleagues. Strong relationships and numerous contacts can provide you with the emotional, practical, and professional support you will need through the ups and downs of start-up.

Perseverance

> *It's not that I'm so smart, it's just that I stay with problems longer.*
>
> —Albert Einstein

Although initiative is important for an entrepreneur, people who are only good at starting things—not finishing them—are not cut out to be entrepreneurs. An entrepreneur's business will likely grow slowly, and the ability to follow through despite obstacles is an important key to success. Success as an entrepreneur will be difficult for those who tend to procrastinate or give up when they don't see results quickly.

The responsibility that comes with starting a paralegal business can be overwhelming, and being able to deal productively with the inevitable frustrations—and to find solutions to problems in a calm, level-headed manner—is essential.

For paralegals, sticking with problems until they are solved is not just a wise business practice, but with respect to work for clients, is an ethical obligation. A paralegal who enters into a retainer with a client is ethically obligated to continue to represent that client unless withdrawal from representation can be justified in accordance with the Rules. Managing client expectations by honestly and fairly discussing the likely risks and costs of clients' matters is important to the business success of paralegal entrepreneurs.

Although some entrepreneurs start their small businesses in part to achieve a better work/life balance—for example, out of a desire to spend more time with their families—many must consistently work long hours to achieve their goals. Seeing tasks through to their conclusions is a process that takes time.

PURPOSE AND OVERVIEW

As a student in a legal services program today, you are preparing to begin your career at an exciting moment in the history of the provision of legal services in Ontario. As a licensed paralegal, you will assume and be required to meet significant professional responsibilities, and will have the chance to benefit from historically unrivalled opportunities.

Only those paralegals who practice ethically and professionally, and who gain and apply sound business knowledge, will profit from the current opportunities. It is the hope of the author that *you* do. The purpose of this book is to allow you to explore and discuss issues that you should consider if you are thinking about starting your own paralegal practice, and to provide you with the basic tools you will need if you decide to do so.

Part I of this book deals with small business issues.

Chapter 2 compares the advantages and challenges of starting a new business from scratch with purchasing an existing business.

Chapter 3 explores regulatory and legal issues related to starting a business. It explains the different forms a business may take (including sole proprietorship, partnership, and professional corporation), the obligations of paralegals with respect to compliance with both the Canadian and Ontario business laws and regulations and the relevant LSUC rules, and the requirements for registering business names. It also looks at issues regarding taxes, licences, zoning, home offices, and insurance.

Chapter 4 outlines what is involved in planning for the start-up of a business. It discusses customer and market profiling, market analysis, and the development of a marketing plan. It also considers financial analysis (including analysis of start-up costs and cash flow), management plans (including their implementation), and the development of a business plan.

Chapter 5 looks at what is involved in maintaining a small business. Relevant rules—such as those relating to business communications, advertising, and setting fees—are explored. As well, the chapter considers personnel management (including issues relating to the hiring and termination of employees, and setting policies) and client retention strategies.

Part II deals with professional practice and compliance issues.

Chapter 6 addresses practice management through an exploration of general obligations, professional responsibility, financial responsibilities, bookkeeping and record keeping, supervisory responsibilities, and delegation.

Chapter 7 considers paralegals' professional obligations when dealing with clients and the public, and explores supervisory responsibility and delegation within this context. The chapter also describes and analyzes the duty to the client; rules limiting advertising, firm names, letterheads, and signs; errors and omissions insurance; and fees and retainers.

Chapter 8 focuses on file management. Confidentiality is considered within this context, and management tools and the organization of file contents are discussed. Recommendations are made to help you comply with LSUC rules regarding management of client property, and closing and storage of inactive files. The chapter also deals with appropriate uses of technology. Time management is reviewed within this context, as are checklists and tickler systems, docketing, and communicating with clients.

KEY TERMS

entrepreneur

Law Society of Upper Canada (LSUC)

legal services

paralegal

USEFUL URLS

Business Development Bank of Canada. "Entrepreneurial Self-Assessment." http://www.bdc.ca/en/business_tools/entrepreneurial_self-Assessment/ Entrepreneurial_self_assessment.htm?cookie%5Ftest=2.

Law Society of Upper Canada (LSUC). "Paralegal Regulation." http://www.lsuc.on.ca/paralegals.

Law Society of Upper Canada (LSUC). 2007, as amended. "Paralegal Rules of Conduct." http://www.lsuc.on.ca/paralegals/a/paralegal-rules-of-conduct.

Law Society of Upper Canada (LSUC). 2008. "Paralegal Professional Conduct Guidelines." http://www.lsuc.on.ca/paralegals/a/paralegal-professional-conduct-guidelines.

Small Business: Canada. "Starting a Business Quiz." http://sbinfocanada.about.com/library/startbusinessquiz/blquestion1.htm.

Ward, Susan. Small Business: Canada. "Doing Credit Checks Can Really Pay Off." http://sbinfocanada.about.com/cs/management/a/creditcheck.htm.

REFERENCES

CIBC World Markets Inc. "Secrets to Small Business Success." 2004. http://www.cibc.com/ca/pdf/sb-secrets-for-success-en.pdf.

Girard, K. "Why Small Businesses Fail: A New Study Adds Insights." 2007. http://www.allbusiness.com/4057970-1.html.

Law Society Act, R.S.O. 1990, c. L.8, as amended.

REVIEW QUESTIONS

1. What is the definition of a "paralegal" in Ontario?

2. What is the LSUC and what is its role with respect to the paralegal profession?

3. To whom do paralegals have obligations and where are these obligations described?

4. What are some traits of entrepreneurs?

CHAPTER 2

Methods of Starting a Business

CHAPTER OBJECTIVES

After completing this chapter, you should be able to:

- Compare the advantages and challenges of opening a new business with those of purchasing an existing business.
- Distinguish between purchasing the assets of a business and purchasing a corporation.

STARTING A NEW BUSINESS

There are advantages as well as challenges associated with building a new business from scratch. Doing so involves a great deal of planning, including the development of a comprehensive business plan; the identification of customers, market potential, and start-up costs; and the formulation of financial projections (discussed in Chapter 4). It is also necessary to determine what form the business should take (see Chapter 3).

Although the amount of planning required can seem daunting, starting a new business allows entrepreneurs to be inventive and creative, and to build something entirely new. Those who build their businesses from scratch are free to shape it however they choose, within the scope of the regulatory context and the law. There is great personal satisfaction in knowing that you have developed a business independently, from the ground up.

Another advantage of building a business from scratch may be a lower initial cost; purchasing an existing business will likely involve more expenditure, or at least more spending all at once.

It may be possible to start a new business on a part-time basis, "moonlighting" from a paying job with another business association and building your commitment to the new business over time. Working for someone else in a business similar to the one you wish to start can provide you with valuable knowledge and experience, but you must ensure that you are not competing unfairly or illegally with your employer. The Rules—in particular, those regarding conflicts of interest—impose constraints on what other work paralegals may take on.

PURCHASING AN EXISTING BUSINESS

For many entrepreneurs, and especially for paralegals, there are a number of reasons why it may make sense to purchase an existing business rather than to start a new one.

Purchasing an existing business—for example, from a paralegal who is preparing to retire—will usually require less planning than starting from scratch, since much of the planning required for a successful business will already have been done. The market for the services will have been tested and demonstrated. Existing legal services businesses are often sold with their client bases, meaning that a group of clients has already been established (although clients remain free to take their business elsewhere). Income levels for the business will be set and will probably be reasonably predictable.

goodwill
an intangible asset consisting of a business's reputation, competitive advantage, and brand, measured by the fair market value of the business less its book value

An existing business will likely have a reputation on which to build. Over time, businesses build up **goodwill**—an intangible asset that can be bought and sold with the business. A business's goodwill is the difference in the value of its assets (minus liabilities) and the market value of the company. It is the amount, in excess of a business's asset value, that a reasonable purchaser could be expected to pay for the entity as a whole—in other words, it is the value of the business's reputation and brand.

Many existing businesses will have employees who wish to continue working with the organization after the new owner purchases it. Their expertise and experience can help ease the ownership transition, preserving client relationships and the flow of business income.

Despite the advantages outlined above, the decision to buy an existing business should only be made after considerable thought and investigation. Moreover, because of the high initial costs, not everyone will have the option of purchasing an existing business. Significant capital—or at least substantial credit—will be required. Over and above the purchase price, it is also likely that several months' worth of working capital will be required to ensure the business has adequate cash flow.

Any business purchase should include a consideration of whether or not the ability of the previous owner to compete with the purchaser will be limited. For example, if a paralegal sells her business to you, is there a written agreement preventing her from setting up an office next door and soliciting customers away? The purchase and sale agreement should include provisions for non-competition and non-solicitation of clients.

The sellers of a business will often be willing to give advice to the purchasers. Some sellers will offer this advice for free, especially if the purchase price is paid over time; in this case, the seller will have an interest in seeing that the business succeeds under its new ownership. In other instances, sellers will provide the business advice for a fee, and this consulting arrangement may be included in the purchase agreement.

Rather than buying a business from another paralegal, you may be able to join a partnership of paralegals. This is common practice in law firms. After working at a law firm for a number of years as an employee, a lawyer may be offered the opportunity to become a partner. This model may be adopted by paralegals operating in partnership, as it allows them to gain experience and expertise with a secure paycheque before acquiring an ownership interest.

Due Diligence

The term **due diligence** is used to refer to the investigation of a business, a person, or the performance of an act in accordance with a particular accepted **standard of care**. When considering the purchase of a paralegal business, you are legally obligated to make reasonable inquiries and investigate the business entity carefully. You should scrutinize the business's legal, financial, staffing, tax, information technology, and market situations. Consulting with the LSUC to determine whether or not there are any outstanding complaints against the practice is also a good idea.

Prospective purchasers should look closely at the business's debts and potential liabilities. **Liabilities** are obligations of persons or entities that arise from past events or transactions—for example, debts or financial obligations. Are there contracts that will involve ongoing obligation or payments that you as the new owner will have to honour? Purchasers should examine finances carefully to determine whether or not there are outstanding debts, and should consider taxes and other obligations to ensure that payments are up to date. Regulatory and legal compliance issues are also important. Purchasers should investigate whether or not the business is in breach of any law or if there are any pending lawsuits.

It is also wise to consider why the current owner is selling the business. Prospective purchasers should try to find out whether or not the business has been neglected; an anonymous visit in person can provide valuable insight into this question. Because reputation is extremely important to a paralegal's business, you should also consider the business's reputation and whether this will be an advantage or a disadvantage to your operation. To do this, it will be helpful to consult with other professionals in the industry.

Prospective purchasers should consider staffing issues. When a corporation is sold, all employment contracts with the corporation as employer continue to exist, and the new owner becomes responsible for termination pay if he chooses to fire anyone. If there are long-term employees that the purchaser does not wish to keep, termination pay can amount to a substantial liability.

In the case of a sale of a **sole proprietorship**—that is, a business owned by a single individual, where there is no legal distinction between the owner of the business and the business itself—all employment contracts are automatically terminated and the seller is responsible for paying termination pay to all employees. This is because the sole proprietor was the employer—only in the case of a corporation is there a separate business entity that continues to employ the same staff. Employment contracts may not legally be assigned (or transferred) from the sole proprietor to the purchaser of the business. The seller must therefore pay termination pay to the employees, who may then negotiate new employment agreements with the purchaser.

In much the same way that a business's clients may choose to take their business elsewhere, employees may quit their jobs at any time. A purchaser cannot assume that employees or clients will remain loyal to the business after a transfer of ownership.

due diligence
investigation of a business or a person, or the performance of an act to ensure compliance with legal or other standards

standard of care
the level of care, competence, or prudence required to avoid liability for negligence

liabilities
debts and other financial obligations

sole proprietorship
a business owned by a single individual, where there is no legal distinction between the owner of the business and the business itself

ASSET PURCHASE

asset
item of value owned by a
company or person,
including tangible items
such as buildings and
equipment, and intangible
ones such as telephone
numbers and licences

asset sale
a sale in which a business's
tangible assets are sold,
but not its name, corporate
identity, and goodwill

Determining precisely what is being offered for sale is another important part of assessing the cost of purchasing an existing business. A business's **assets** include items of value that may be tangible, such as buildings or equipment, or intangible, such as business name, goodwill, telephone numbers or licences. In an **asset sale**, only a business's tangible assets are sold; this does not include the business's name, work in progress, and goodwill. While asset sales are much more common in the manufacturing sector, where there is substantial machinery and equipment to sell, it is still important to be clear on what is being purchased in any business sale. If *only* the assets are purchased, the purchaser will not be obtaining work in progress and goodwill.

If the purchase is an asset sale, the purchase and sale documents should include a detailed account of what assets are being sold. A meticulous list should be made of all of the physical objects—for example, the photocopier, desks, chairs, customer lists, and telephones. Purchasers should think carefully about what fair value for assets is; equipment offered for sale may be obsolete. If you wish to purchase used office equipment and furniture at a discounted price, you may be better off searching websites such as Craigslist and Kijiji for the specific items you need.

PRICE

A potential purchaser of an existing paralegal business should be very careful when negotiating the purchase price, and should consider hiring a professional to help determine what a reasonable value is. An appraiser can provide an estimated fair market value of assets, including any depreciation in the value of equipment or other assets. A business valuator can calculate more complex issues, such as future earning potential.

CONCLUSION

Paralegals who wish to start businesses as providers of legal services can choose to start their businesses from scratch or decide to purchase an existing business. Both options involve their own unique advantages and challenges. Although starting a business from scratch requires a great deal of planning, it allows entrepreneurs to be inventive and creative, and can be deeply rewarding. On the other hand, while paralegals who purchase an existing business have less planning and uncertainty to deal with and have the business' existing reputation on which to build, not everyone can afford the high initial costs. Prospective buyers should investigate the business very carefully.

Purchasing a corporation is not the same as purchasing that corporation's assets, and potential buyers should find out what exactly is being offered for sale when assessing the costs of purchasing an existing business. When negotiating a purchase price for a corporation and/or its assets, potential purchasers should consider hiring a professional to help them determine what a reasonable value is.

KEY TERMS

asset

asset sale

due diligence

goodwill

liabilities

sole proprietorship

standard of care

USEFUL URLS

Artim, Greg. "Purchasing an Existing Business—Legal Dos and Don'ts."
http://ezinearticles.com/?Purchasing-an-Existing-Business---Legal-Dos-
and-Donts&id=509495.

Business Link. "Buy an Existing Business." http://www.businesslink.gov.uk/bdotg/
action/detail?type=RESOURCES&itemId=1074410852.

CanadaOne. 2005. "Starting a Business in Canada." http://www.canadaone.com/
tools/startingabusiness.html.

Law Society of Upper Canada (LSUC). 2007, as amended. "Paralegal Rules of
Conduct." http://www.lsuc.on.ca/paralegals/a/paralegal-rules-of-conduct.

REVIEW QUESTIONS

1. Describe some advantages of starting a new business as opposed to taking
    over an existing one.

2. Describe some advantages of purchasing an existing business.

3. What is goodwill?

4. What is due diligence?

5. What is an asset sale?

CHAPTER 3

Regulatory and Legal Start-Up Issues

CHAPTER OBJECTIVES

After completing this chapter, you should be able to:

- Understand the different methods of conducting business as a paralegal, including in the form of a sole proprietorship, a partnership, and a professional corporation.

- Explain the advantages and disadvantages of operating a sole proprietorship.

- Explain the advantages and disadvantages of conducting business in a partnership.

- Explain the advantages and disadvantages of conducting business as part of a corporation.

- Identify when registration of a business name is necessary.

- Explain the advantages and disadvantages of home offices.

- Understand the importance of insurance for paralegals and know what type of insurance is mandatory.

BUSINESS FORMS

When starting a business, you will need to decide what form your business will take. You may decide to operate as a sole proprietorship, a partnership, or a professional corporation. Each form entails unique advantages and disadvantages.

Sole Proprietorship

A sole proprietorship is the simplest form that a business can take. Sole proprietorships are relatively easy to set up, to wind up, or to terminate. The only legal rules for setting up a sole proprietorship involve business name registration and business licensing. Business law does not provide any particular rules for the set-up or dissolution of a sole proprietorship.

Despite the relatively simple and informal set-up procedures involved, sole proprietorships have their disadvantages—primarily, unlimited personal liability. A sole proprietor is personally liable for any debts incurred by the business. This means that paralegals operating as sole proprietors can lose personal assets, such as their cars or homes, and be forced into personal bankruptcy if sued successfully or if unable to pay their business debts.

Sole proprietors are personally responsible for performing all obligations incurred in the course of the operation of their businesses. In addition, they bear exclusive responsibility for any and all civil or criminal wrongs they commit in the course of operating their businesses, and can be held personally responsible for acts committed by their employees in the course of their work. The liabilities of paralegal sole proprietors include (but are not limited to) occupier's liability with respect to any injuries that occur on the premises, such as slip and fall, and professional liability for any harm caused to a client as a result of errors or omissions made by the paralegal or her employees.

Partnership

partnership
a form of business in which two or more persons carry on business together with a reasonable expectation of a profit; also called a general partnership

A **partnership** (also called a general partnership) is a form of business practice in which two or more persons carry on business together with a reasonable expectation of making a profit. Generally, the partners in a partnership all share in the profits or losses of their endeavour. Like sole proprietorships, partnerships are relatively easy to create and wind up.

The *Partnerships Act* makes clear that a partnership is considered to exist whenever two or more persons or entities find themselves in a business relationship like the one described above. In many cases, courts have found partnerships to exist even where this was not the intention of the parties involved.

The *Partnerships Act* provides rules that, by default, govern the relationship between partners—for example, that all partners are equal. However, partners may create partnership agreements, overriding these rules by making their own agreements about how to carry on their businesses. A partnership agreement might, for example, specify that profits and losses will be distributed among partners unequally (and describe how), or that only some partners have a role in managing the partnership. Any changes to a partnership agreement require the partners' unanimous consent.

Like a sole proprietorship, a partnership is a *method* of conducting business but it is not legally a business *entity*—meaning that it has no legal existence apart from the existence of the individual partners. In general, and like sole proprietors, partners in a business bear personal liability for all obligations entered into on behalf of the partnership. Any contracts signed or debts owed by the partnership become *personal obligations* of each partner. Lawsuits may be commenced against the partnership, and any court judgment may be collected from each and all partners personally. This kind of liability, known as **joint and several liability**, is one of the main risks and potential disadvantages of the partnership business form.

joint and several liability
shared liability, such that all parties are equally liable for the full amount of the debt or obligation

fiduciary duty
an obligation, with respect to financial matters, to put the interests of the person owed the duty above one's own interests

Because of joint and several liability, trust between the partners in a partnership is very important. Partners have a **fiduciary duty** to one another, which requires them to act with honesty and in good faith, protecting each other's interests very carefully.

In addition to the kind of partnership described above, two other types of partnerships exist: limited partnerships and limited liability partnerships. **Limited partnerships**, which are governed by the *Limited Partnerships Act*, allow the partners to limit or restrict liability to only some of the partners. This may be useful if a partnership is seeking investment by a "silent partner" who will not take an active role in the business.

In order to take advantage of the special rules that apply to limited partners, you must file specific forms and information with the government. Limited partnerships must also be identified as such to the public. Finally, limited partners can forfeit the limits on their liability if they participate in the management of their firms.

The third type of partnership, known as a **limited liability partnership**, is governed by the *Partnerships Act*. Used by many professionals, the main advantage of these partnerships is that they offer limited liability with respect to the professional negligence of other partners. This means that if one partner is successfully sued for professional negligence the other partners are *not* jointly and severally liable for the amount of the judgment; only with respect to other types of business debts and obligations, such as non-payment of rent or occupier's liability, are the partners jointly and severally liable. The name of a limited liability partnership must be registered under the *Business Names Act* and must include the words "limited liability partnership" or the abbreviation "LLP." This is to notify the public that the partners are not jointly and severally liable for professional negligence.

The LSUC permits paralegals to operate in limited liability partnerships, and such partnerships are common in the legal services industry. By-law 7 requires that all partners in a limited liability partnership maintain their own professional liability insurance coverage in accordance with By-law 6.

limited partnership
a type of partnership that restricts liability to only one or some of the partners, as set out in a partnership agreement

limited liability partnership
a partnership of professionals where not all of the partners are liable for the professional negligence of one or some of the partners

Corporation

Although lawyers have traditionally carried out their business in partnerships, an increasing number of legal services providers are forming corporations. A **corporation** is a business organization that has a legal existence separate and apart from that of the individuals who created it or who operate it.

Corporations are characterized by a specific and required division of powers. They are owned collectively by shareholders, who are entitled to a share of corporate assets. Shareholders elect directors to manage the corporation, appointing and hiring officers. Officers are the employees of a corporation; they are responsible for its operation on a day-to-day basis. The same individual(s) can act in all three capacities (shareholder, director, and officer), but the titles and roles of each position remain distinct.

The primary advantages of corporations are flexibility and limited liability. Flexibility results from the fact that the owners of the business can change without altering the business itself; contracts and staffing, among other things, remain in place through changes in ownership. Regarding limited liability, in general the owners (shareholders) of a corporation are not personally liable for the debts and liabilities of the corporation. This means that only the assets owned by the corporation may be used to satisfy its liabilities, not the owners' personal assets.

corporation
a business entity that has a legal existence separate and apart from that of the individuals who created it or who operate it

PROFESSIONAL CORPORATIONS

Paralegals and lawyers who wish to provide legal services in Ontario may do so through a particular kind of corporation called a **professional corporation**. Professional corporations must hold a valid certificate of authorization as outlined in the *Law Society Act* and By-law 7, and are governed by certain rules.

Most significantly, the *Law Society Act* imposes personal liability in certain circumstances on individuals who practise within professional corporations. Sections 3.1 to 3.4 of the Act set out a framework under which professionals are required to perform tasks diligently and may be personally liable for failing to meet the appropriate standard. In this way, professional corporations are similar to limited liability partnerships—while professional corporations will protect the shareholder-owners against liability for general debts or liability, such as a slip and fall on the premises, they will not protect them against liability for professional negligence, such as missing a limitation period. This exception preserves accountability and protects clients.

Unlike a partnership or sole proprietorship, a corporation does not automatically come into being but must be "incorporated"—that is, created by a prescribed legal process set out in statute and in regulations. Corporations may be created under the federal corporate law statute, the *Canada Business Corporations Act* or under provincial ones. In Ontario, the relevant statute is the *Business Corporations Act*.

Although advantageous to entrepreneurs because of the limited liability they provide, corporations are more complex to set up and maintain than partnerships or sole proprietorships. Those who own, direct, or operate corporations must file annual reports, and shareholders must hold periodic meetings to elect directors. As a result of the different individuals and procedures involved, entrepreneurs will generally have less control over a corporation than over a sole proprietorship.

LSUC REQUIREMENTS

In addition to ensuring compliance with the laws and regulations that apply to all Canadian and Ontario businesses, paralegals must comply with the LSUC rules for choosing a business form and starting their businesses outlined in By-law 7. For example, paralegals who operate limited liability partnerships must identify their partnerships as such, and each partner must carry professional liability insurance in accordance with By-law 6. Corporations that provide legal services are regulated, "professional" corporations whose names are governed by s. 3; for example, only companies that include several licensed professionals may use the term "and associates." Paralegals may apply to the LSUC for a certificate stating that the Society does not object to a particular proposed corporate name (ss. 4(1) and (2)).

By-law 7 (s. 5) requires corporations seeking to provide legal services in Ontario to apply for, and obtain from the LSUC, a certificate authorizing them to do so. There are certain conditions of receiving a certificate, including a requirement that the corporation is in compliance with the *Business Corporations Act* and that all individuals who will be providing legal services on behalf of the corporation are properly licensed with the LSUC.

Paralegals whose businesses do not comply with LSUC certificate and other requirements risk losing their licences.

FINDING INFORMATION

Paralegals must be familiar with the Rules, the Guidelines, the LSUC by-laws, and all other regulations that apply to their businesses. Continuing education through legal education seminars is recommended to keep your professional knowledge in these areas current. You can also find information regarding incorporation, corporate filings, tax matters, and so on online. Use only official websites, such as government websites or the LSUC's website. The LSUC maintains a "Paralegal Questions & Answers" page, which includes telephone numbers and an email address to help you obtain answers to any questions you may have.

BUSINESS NAME REGISTRATION

Ontario's *Business Names Act* requires the names of sole proprietorships to be registered only where these differ from the legal name of the sole proprietor. For example, if your name is Frank Oz and you operate under "Frank Oz, Paralegal," no registration is required. However, if you wish to operate as "Frank's Legal Services," you must register this name or risk fines.

Partnerships must register their business' names where these are not simply a list of the partners' names. Because the names of corporations are registered at the time of incorporation, corporations are not required to do a separate name registration.

TAXES

When choosing a form for your business, you should consider the treatment of each form by the income tax laws of Canada. Tax issues can affect the profitability of a business significantly.

As noted, in a sole proprietorship there is no legal distinction between the owner of the business and the business itself. Therefore, on their personal income tax returns, sole proprietors include the profits or losses of their business along with their income from any other sources. Similarly, because a partnership has no separate legal existence from that of the partners, each partner reports his or her share of the partnership's profits on his or her personal income tax return.

Incorporating a business entails tax advantages. Corporations are taxed separately from their owners, and in general the corporate tax rate is significantly lower than the individual tax rate. However, there are costs associated with obtaining this lower tax rate. The Canadian Revenue Agency can provide information and assistance regarding tax issues with respect to corporations, but it is advisable for the owners of a corporation to enlist the services of an accountant to ensure that income taxes are filed properly and that the appropriate financial records are maintained. Finally, monies paid to shareholders as dividends or to officers or directors in remuneration—for example, in the form of salaries or bonuses—are taxable as income to the individuals who receive them.

ANNUAL FILING WITH THE LSUC

By-law 8 (s. 5) requires all licensed paralegals to submit an annual report to the LSUC each year before March 31 (to submit a report, visit https://eforms.lsuc.on.ca). The report asks paralegals to provide details regarding their provision of legal services, as well as financial activities, during the relevant year. There is no fee for filing. Failure to comply in a timely manner may result in suspension by the LSUC.

LICENCES

In addition to the LSUC's licensing requirements for paralegals, additional business licensing requirements may apply to businesses in particular provinces or municipalities. All businesses in Ontario are subject to licensing laws, and each municipal government has the authority to issue business licences within its geographic area or jurisdiction.

    If you wish to operate a business, you are responsible for determining which local by-laws, regulations, and other rules will affect your business. The best way to find out is by contacting the clerk of the municipality in which your business will operate. You can find telephone numbers on the appropriate municipal government's website or in the telephone directory's blue pages.

ZONING AND BUILDING

Zoning refers to the legal use of property. Zoning laws can limit where legal services businesses may operate and set conditions for their operation. The Canada–Ontario Business Service Centre provides useful information regarding the municipal requirements for starting a business, including the applicability of zoning laws. Prospective paralegal entrepreneurs in Ontario should consult with their local municipal governments to determine what zoning laws may apply to them. There may also be by-laws that apply to signage and parking.

    In addition to zoning laws, Ontario's municipalities administer laws and regulations with regard to buildings. The Building Code governs both the construction of new buildings and the maintenance and renovation of existing ones, including office premises.

THE HOME OFFICE

The increasing use of technology in the provision of legal services has made law-related professions more portable, and home-based businesses are viable options for more legal services providers. Operating a business from home has many appealing aspects. You will save significantly on overhead costs, especially at the outset, and will not have to spend time commuting. In addition, you can claim a portion of your household expenses—such as heating and mortgage payments—against your business income for income tax purposes.

However, home offices have their disadvantages, such as encroachment on personal time and space; the fact that it may be more difficult to "leave" work may increase stress levels. There may also be safety issues with respect to clients visiting you at home. It may be possible to rent boardroom space for this purpose on an as-needed basis in a local office building or a public library.

Before setting up a home office, you may wish to confirm that small home businesses are allowed by the zoning by-laws in your neighbourhood. You should also update your home insurance policy to ensure coverage of your business assets.

INSURANCE

The LSUC requires paralegals who practise in Ontario to carry errors and omissions insurance. At the time of writing, paralegals must carry $1 million in liability insurance and $2 million in aggregate liability insurance (where there are multiple claims). Visit the LSUC's website for a list of providers who meet the LSUC requirements.

You will also need to insure your premises and the contents of your office, and obtain occupier's liability insurance to protect you in the event that anyone is injured while at your office. If you are renting office space, your lease agreement will set out the insurance coverage required by your landlord. Your insurer will likely ask for a copy of your lease in order to ensure that you are purchasing appropriate coverage.

You may wish to consider purchasing business interruption insurance, which will provide you with compensation in the event that you are unable to operate for a period of time as a result of a fire or other calamity. Finally, as a self-employed person, you should consider purchasing health and dental, life, and—most importantly—disability insurance, for both yourself and any employees.

CONCLUSION

Paralegals may conduct their business in the form of a sole proprietorship, in one of the three forms of partnerships (general partnership, limited partnership, or limited liability partnership), or in the form of a professional corporation. Each business form carries advantages and disadvantages, and each is governed by different legislation, including federal and provincial laws and regulations. By-law 7 outlines LSUC requirements for different business entities.

Although relatively simple to set up and wind down, among other disadvantages sole proprietorships entail unlimited personal liability, meaning that sole proprietors can lose personal assets if unable to pay their business debts.

In partnerships, two or more persons carry on business together with a reasonable expectation of making a profit. Sharing marketing, premises, and staff allows them to conduct their business with greater efficiency. Like sole proprietors, partners bear personal liability for all obligations entered into on behalf of the partnership. They may be held jointly and severally liable in any court judgments, including claims of professional negligence.

Partners in a limited partnership can limit or restrict liability to only some of the partners. Limited liability partnerships offer limited liability with respect to the professional negligence of partners, meaning that if one partner is successfully sued the other partners are not jointly and severally liable for the amount of the judgment.

Paralegals and lawyers who wish to operate professional corporations must obtain a valid certificate of authorization from the LSUC. The *Law Society Act* imposes personal liability in certain circumstances on individuals who practise within professional corporations—they must perform tasks diligently and may be personally liable for failing to meet the appropriate standard.

Operating your business from home will save you money and time in overhead costs and commuting, but a home office may encroach on your personal time and space, and raise safety concerns with respect to client visits. Regardless of the type of business you operate or where you operate from, you will require errors and omissions insurance and should consider what additional types of insurance—such as occupier's liability insurance, and life, health and dental, and disability coverage—you may require or may wish to obtain.

KEY TERMS

corporation

fiduciary duty

joint and several liability

limited liability partnership

limited partnership

partnership

professional corporation

USEFUL URLS

Building Code, O. Reg. 350/06.

Business Corporations Act, R.S.O. 1990, c. B.16. http://www.e-laws.gov.on.ca/html/statutes/english/elaws_statutes_90b16_e.htm

Business Names Act, R.S.O. 1990, c. B.17. http://www.e-laws.gov.on.ca/html/statutes/english/elaws_statutes_90b17_e.htm.

Canada Business Corporations Act, R.S.C. 1985, c. C-44. http://laws.justice.gc.ca/en/C-44/index.html.

Canada–Ontario Business Service Centre. http://www.bsc-sec.ca/servlet/ContentServer?cid=1183551597162&pagename=CBSC_ON/CBSC_WebPage/CBSC_WebPage_Temp&lang=en&c=CBSC_WebPage.

Industry Canada. 2009. Corporations Canada. "Chapter 1—Why Should I Incorporate?" http://www.ic.gc.ca/eic/site/cd-dgc.nsf/eng/cs01357.html.

Law Society of Upper Canada (LSUC). "Paralegal Questions & Answers." http://www.lsuc.on.ca/paralegals/a/paralegal-questions-answers.

Law Society of Upper Canada (LSUC). 2005. "By-Laws." http://www.lsuc.on.ca/
regulation/a/by-laws.

Law Society of Upper Canada (LSUC). 2007, as amended. "Paralegal Rules of
Conduct." http://www.lsuc.on.ca/paralegals/a/paralegal-rules-of-conduct.

Law Society of Upper Canada (LSUC). 2008. "Paralegal Professional Conduct
Guidelines." http://www.lsuc.on.ca/paralegals/a/paralegal-professional-
conduct-guidelines.

Limited Partnerships Act, R.S.O. 1990, c. L.16. http://www.e-laws.gov.on.ca/html/
statutes/english/elaws_statutes_90l16_e.htm.

Ministry of Municipal Affairs and Housing. 2009. "Ontario Building Code."
http://www.obc.mah.gov.on.ca/site4.aspx.

Paralegal Society of Ontario. http://www.paralegalsociety.on.ca/index.php.

Partnerships Act, R.S.O. 1990, c. P.5. http://www.e-laws.gov.on.ca/html/statutes/
english/elaws_statutes_90p05_e.htm.

REFERENCES

Business Names Act, R.S.O. 1990, c. B.17.

Law Society Act, R.S.O. 1990, c. L.8, as amended.

Law Society of Upper Canada (LSUC). "By-Laws." 2005. http://www.lsuc.on.ca/
regulation/a/by-laws.

Limited Partnerships Act, R.S.O. 1990, c. L.16.

Partnerships Act, R.S.O. 1990, c. P.5.

REVIEW QUESTIONS

1. What is a sole proprietorship?
2. What is a partnership?
3. What is a corporation?
4. What is a professional corporation?
5. Can you name your business anything you want? What limitations exist?

CHAPTER 4

Planning for Start-Up

CHAPTER OBJECTIVES

After completing this chapter, you should be able to:

- Create a business plan.
- Understand the purpose of client and market profiles and how to develop these.
- Understand the purpose of market analysis and a marketing plan.
- Understand basic principles of sound financial planning and analysis, including start-up costs and cash flow analysis.
- Create a management plan.
- Strategize for effective implementation of plans.

BUSINESS PLAN

A **business plan** is a document that contains a summary of a business's operational and financial objectives, along with detailed plans and budgets that explain how the objectives will be achieved. A business plan is for a paralegal business what architectural plans are for a building; few people would ride an elevator to the top of the CN Tower if the building had not been expertly engineered. Legal services entrepreneurs should consider consulting professionals and should look carefully at available sources of start-up funding when developing their business plans. A detailed and realistic business plan makes planning a business more manageable and more effective.

Business plans evolve as new information is gathered and as circumstances change, but having a detailed framework prior to start-up is important. A business plan can test the practicality of a business idea; it is a risk-free rehearsal for opening the business. Because they allow flaws to be identified and corrected (or at least minimized) before implementation, business plans can provide huge savings in time and money. The alternative process of trial and error can be extremely costly.

A detailed business plan is also useful for acquiring capital from third parties. Banks more readily grant loans, and investors are more willing to become involved in a business that has detailed plans available for their review and assessment.

business plan
a document that contains a summary of a business's operational and financial objectives, along with detailed plans and budgets that explain how the objectives will be achieved

The components of business plans vary, but generally include

- client and market profiles;

- market analysis;

- the business's mission;

- a marketing plan;

- an operating plan (detailing location, facilities, equipment, and staff);

- a financial plan;

- appendixes (incorporation documents, resumés of key management players, leases for office space and equipment, the licences of paralegals providing legal services, shareholder or partnership agreements, copies of academic credentials, and so on); and

- milestones (objectives, goals, and action plans with dates).

Your business plan should be specific and detailed enough to allow you to make financially sound decisions and take reasonable risks.

CLIENT AND MARKET PROFILES

client profile
data relating to the demographics of a business's potential clients—such as their geographic location, age, income level, gender, ethnicity, and education level—that allows business owners to assess the needs of their target market

An important way to assess opportunities for your business's future success is by creating client and market profiles. A **client profile** is data relating to the demographics of your potential clients, such as:

- geographic location

- age

- income level

- gender

- ethnicity

- education level.

The client profile will allow you to assess the needs of your target market. It can help you understand who your clients will likely be, how to find them, and how to motivate them to purchase your services. For example, if your clients are renters, they may need representation with respect to landlord and tenant matters; if they are immigrants, they may need immigration advice.

market profile
a business tool, created through research, that provides business owners with important information about areas of opportunity in the market—for example, common legal problems in a particular market

A **market profile** can provide you with important information about areas of opportunity in the market. For example, what types of legal problems are common? Which areas are served poorly by lawyers (for example, due to the high price of services)? Are these areas within the scope of permitted practice for paralegals? This information may help you design your website, choose the most effective advertising media, fine-tune your marketing strategies, and determine prices for your services.

Client and market profiles are created through research. Telephone or online surveys can be useful research methods in the case of ongoing businesses, and employees may be able to compile the relevant data themselves. Once the likely target group of clients is defined, that information can be cross-referenced with information known about that particular demographic subgroup. For example, if you are providing traffic law advice primarily and your typical clients are middle-class males with a college education located in a particular neighbourhood, you will want to consider what kind of advertising will appeal to them, such as ads in the autotrader, newspaper, or media relating to sports in the area.

MARKET ANALYSIS

Market analysis is used by business owners—in the planning stages of their business and on an ongoing basis—to help them determine the opportunities and risks of a particular market and how these may affect their success. A typical market analysis considers the following factors:

- Market growth rate: The market growth rate for future years can be extrapolated from an analysis of the growth rate in the market in past year; although not definitive, information about the past is useful for making projections.

- Market size: The size of your market can be estimated based on information obtained from Statistics Canada and your local chamber of commerce. Your own surveys may also be helpful.

- Market profitability: Can your target market afford legal services? How many will qualify for legal aid? Income information may be available from Statistics Canada. You can also visit neighbourhoods in person to assess socio-economic levels.

- Market trends: Be aware of changes to the law or demographics that may affect your business or present new opportunities. Examples include the substantial monetary increase in the maximum jurisdiction of the Small Claims Court set to take place in 2010, which will cause the number of small claims cases to rise; the particular legal services needs of an aging population; and language barriers of a new immigrant group. Keep up to date with trends by monitoring local and legal news.

market analysis
used by business owners, in the planning stages of their business and on an ongoing basis, to help them determine the opportunities and risks of a particular market and how these may affect their success

MARKETING PLAN

A **marketing plan** is a document that sets out actions identified as necessary for a business to achieve the marketing objectives identified through its client and market profiling. The plan should move from general to specific points, first outlining the overall objectives or "mission" of the organization, then setting out specific objectives and action plans. For example, your mission may be to become the most respected legal services provider for a particular neighbourhood, achieving both affordability and quality. Your specific objectives may be to serve new immigrants and low-income members of the community. Action plans may involve advertising in different ethnic newspapers, hiring bilingual staff and promoting this to the public, and offering free legal information at community centres.

marketing plan
a document that sets out actions identified as necessary for a business to achieve its marketing objectives

A marketing plan should identify client groups to be served (usually through client profiling), client needs to be met, and how those needs will be met. A marketing plan for a small legal services business might include the following:

- a description of the specific legal services that will be provided and any aspects of the business that may set it apart, such as unique credentials or past experience of any of the paralegals (for example, former police officers);

- a marketing budget estimate, including a plan for advertising and promotion;

- a description of where the business will be located, and the advantages and disadvantages of that location;

- a strategy for setting fees (for example, billable hours or flat rates for services); and

- client and market profiles.

Marketing plans should be written out, since written documents serve as clear reference points that can be evaluated. Because the market will change and each action may affect other actions, the plans should be treated as works-in-progress and should be revised continuously—for example, if the demographics in your area change or if new advertising opportunities arise.

BUDGETING AND FINANCIAL PLANNING

When starting a business, making financial plans and setting budgets is critical to success. **Financial plans** are a key component of business plans. They provide a framework for measuring money coming into and going out of the business—more specifically, they show how much money is required to operate the business and where that money is coming from.

financial plan
a key component of a business plan that concerns the money coming into and going out of the business; shows how much money is required to operate the business and where that money is coming from

In its most basic form, a **budget** is a list of anticipated or intended income and expenses for a defined future period. Budgets facilitate realistic and accurate financial planning, allowing businesses to set goals for the future and to track and assess achievement of these goals. They can allow for control of growth, some measure of evaluation, and general planning; facilitate communication between individuals within an organization; and motivate individuals to work harder.

budget
a list of anticipated income and expenses for a defined future period

Budgets are typically made for periods of one year; the year period over which a budget runs is the *fiscal* year and does not necessarily coincide with the calendar year. Monthly budget targets may also be set. It is generally a good idea to set annual targets and then break them down by month. In the process of setting your budget, it may be useful to consult an accountant or bookkeeper; otherwise, you will need to acquire basic accounting skills yourself.

cash flow
movement of money into and out of a business

Among other things, budgets predict and record **cash flow**, or the movement of money into and out of a business. To analyze cash flow is to study the cycles through which cash flows in and out. A business's accounts receivable, accounts payable, and credit all affect cash flow analysis.

Many paralegal businesses struggle with cash flow, and it is important to develop systems to ensure that clients pay for the services they receive. Collecting upfront retainers, billing regularly over the course of a file, and accepting payment by credit card are some measures that paralegal businesses can implement to protect against potential cash flow shortages.

Budgeted income for a particular period—namely, client fees paid—must be balanced against the expenditures to be made during the same time period. Expenses may include office rent, telephone, Internet, supplies, insurance, and employee salaries (including your own). In addition to these ongoing expenses, small businesses will likely incur significant one-time start-up costs—for example, purchasing computers and office furniture and paying first and last month's rent. The difference between the income and expenditures is the *profit* or *loss* for the period.

In general, it is wisest to calculate budgets on a cash basis, where only money actually spent or received during the period is included. Particularly where fees are charged for services (for example, in the work of paralegals), businesses must ensure that their budgets distinguish between money still owed to them for fees ("billable" or "billed" fees) and money they have actually received.

Budgets should be set as projections prior to the beginning of a particular period. Once the period ends, actual revenues and expenses should be tracked and compared with the expected or projected numbers. Comparing their budgeted numbers to actual ones can help businesses with their ongoing planning. They can look for explanations for differences between anticipated and actual earnings and expenses, and through this type of **financial analysis** can determine whether they are setting appropriate fees, renting suitable office space, need to add or reduce resources or employees, and so on.

MANAGEMENT PLAN

The **management plan** is the part of a business plan that outlines how the business is structured and describes the responsibilities of various individuals with respect to its management. The plan should not only set out who does what, but why—that is, it should outline how the particular skills and expertise of key individuals will contribute to the business's profitability. For paralegals working together, it is important to assess and understand how the work of each can complement that of the others.

If the business is a sole proprietorship, the management plan will be simple; the sole proprietor will be the decision-maker. However, if the business structure is more complex—as in a partnership or a professional corporation with more than one shareholder—the management plan becomes more critical. In these cases, the plan may include a detailed partnership agreement that sets out the responsibilities and decision-making authority of each partner, or articles of incorporation that name the directors, officers, and shareholders, and outline the responsibilities and decision-making authority of these individuals.

Basic tasks involved in most small businesses include marketing, sales, administration, and business development. Most small businesses will not have a separate individual responsible for each task. The management plan should acknowledge this and should set out the tasks that each individual has been assigned to perform, even where responsibility for a task is shared. The manner in which each member of the management team will be compensated should also be described.

financial analysis
a comparison by a business of its budgeted numbers with actual ones to find explanations for differences between its anticipated and actual earnings and expenses, and to help it determine such things as whether it is setting appropriate fees, renting suitable office space, and so on

management plan
the part of a business plan that outlines how the business is structured and describes the responsibilities of various individuals with respect to its management

STRATEGIZING TO IMPLEMENT PLANS

Once a business has made its plans, it must implement them effectively. In order for plans to become reality, they must be structured in such a way that they can be continuously reviewed and revised. Your business plan will include a statement of goals, objectives, tasks, and action plans. Dates should be set at which the implementation of each of these will be assessed and reassessed.

The management team and the employees need to know what their specific targets are and when these should be met. When these are not met, the reasons why should be investigated. Businesses often devote significant attention to drafting their business plans but fail to pay enough attention to assessing and evaluating to what extent these are being implemented once the business is underway. Reviewing performance and measuring results are important aspects of maintaining a business.

SAMPLE BUSINESS PLAN

ABC Paralegal Professional Corporation—Business Plan

Executive Summary

The objectives of ABC are to generate a profit, to grow at a challenging yet manageable rate, and to be an intellectual and social asset to the community in the service of justice and the public good.

ABC's mission is to provide affordable, fast, and reliable legal assistance to clients in civil matters before the Small Claims Court.

The keys to success for ABC are reputation and networking, responsiveness and quality, and generating repeat and referral clients.

Hourly legal services will be the initial primary service offered by ABC, though contingency contracts and projects will be considered in the future.

There is an existing local market for this business, which our research has shown can support new and expanding legal services firms.

An initial financial analysis of the viability of this venture shows promise.

1.1 Objectives

The objectives of this business plan are to provide both a written guide for starting and managing ABC Paralegal Professional Corporation and a strategic framework for developing a comprehensive tactical marketing plan.

The scope of this plan is to provide detailed monthly projections for the current plan year and yearly summaries for the following two years.

The objectives of ABC Paralegal Professional Corporation are:

- Profit: To generate sufficient profit to finance future growth and to provide the resources needed to achieve the other objectives of the company and of the paralegal owners. (Net profit of at least 25 percent of billings in first year.)

- Growth: To grow the business at a rate that is challenging yet manageable, leading the market with innovation and adapting to the needs of our clients. (Grow from 20 billable hours/week at end of Year 1 to 35 billable hours/week in Year 3.)

- Citizenship: To be an intellectual and social asset to the community, and to serve the interests of justice and the public good. (Each paralegal shall contribute 2 hours per week as volunteer; the company will contribute 1 percent of pre-tax profits to charity.)

(Continued)

(Continued)

1.2 Mission

ABC Paralegal Professional Corporation's mission is simple and straightforward:

- Purpose: ABC exists to provide fast, reliable legal assistance to clients with civil matters within the jurisdiction of the Small Claims Court of Ontario.

- Vision: By providing fast response, informed expertise, and consistently high quality solutions, ABC generates enough satisfied repeat and referral clients to provide a stable retainer base. This generates sufficient profit to provide a comfortable living for the paralegal owners.

- Mission: The short-term objective is to start this company quickly and inexpensively, with a minimum of debt. The long-term objective is to grow it into a stable and profitable business that the paralegal owners can comfortably manage.

- Marketing Slogan: "Legal Problems Made as Easy as ABC!"

1.3 Keys to Success

The keys to success for ABC Paralegal Professional Corporation are:

- Marketing and Networking (getting the name out there)

- Responsiveness (being a reliable and responsive resource for clients)

- Quality (serving clients with professional work of the highest quality and integrity)

- Relationships (developing loyal repeat and referral clients)

ABC Paralegal Professional Corporation will be a start-up venture with the following characteristics:

- ABC will be incorporated in Ontario as a licensed professional corporation in accordance with the relevant LSUC rules and business legislation.

- The goal will be to start the venture as inexpensively as possible, with no debt financing.

- ABC will initially be a home office start-up, utilizing two studio rooms in the paralegal owners' home.

- Client meetings will be held at the courthouse or at clients' homes or places of business.

...

CONCLUSION

Having a detailed framework prior to the start-up of your business in the form of a business plan is important to your business's eventual success. Business plans typically include client and market profiles; market analysis; a statement of the business's mission; marketing, operating, and financial plans; appendixes containing a variety of additional information; and clearly outlined milestones that include objectives, goals, and action plans with dates.

Creating client and market profiles through research will allow you to assess opportunities for the future success of your business. Client profiles allow you to assess the needs of your target market through data relating to the demographics of your potential clients, while market profiles provide important information about areas of opportunity in the market.

Conducting a market analysis is another important aspect of the planning process. Typically, this involves a consideration of the market growth rate, market size, market profitability, and market trends. The information gained from market analysis will help you determine the opportunities and risks of a particular market and how these may affect their success, in the planning stages of your business and on an ongoing basis.

Marketing plans set out actions identified as necessary for a business to achieve the marketing objectives identified through its client and market profiling. They should be written out and, for a small legal services business, should include a description of the specific legal services to be provided; a marketing budget estimate, including a plan for advertising and promotion; a description of where the business will be located, and the advantages and disadvantages of that location; a strategy for setting fees; and client and market profiles.

Budgets are another important planning tool, allowing businesses to set goals for the future and to track and assess achievement of those goals. When setting a budget for your business, you might consider consulting with an accountant or a bookkeeper.

The tasks for which each individual who holds a management position within the organization is responsible should be set out in a management plan. In partnerships and professional corporations, the plan may include a detailed partnership agreement or articles of incorporation. Management plans should also describe the manner in which each member of the management team will be compensated.

Paralegal entrepreneurs must ensure that their plans are implemented effectively once they have been made. This involves setting dates for the assessment and reassessment of whether and how the goals, objectives, tasks, and action plans included in your business plan are being implemented and achieved.

KEY TERMS

budget

business plan

cash flow

client profile

financial analysis

financial plan

management plan

market analysis

market profile

marketing plan

USEFUL URLS

Clark, Jacquel K. 2001. "Keys to Successfully Implementing a Business Plan." http://www.allbusiness.com/business-planning/813472-1.html.

Idea Cafe Inc. "All-in-One First Year Budget Worksheet." http://www.businessownersideacafe.com/financing/budget_calculator.html.

Microsoft Corporation. 2009. Microsoft Small Business Center. "Startups." http://www.microsoft.com/smallbusiness/resources/startups/small-business-startups.aspx.

NetMBA. "Market Analysis." http://www.netmba.com/marketing/market/analysis.

Small Business: Canada. "Business Plans." http://sbinfocanada.about.com/od/businessplans/Business_Plans.htm.

REVIEW QUESTIONS

1. What is a marketing plan?

2. What might some elements of a marketing plan be for a small paralegal business?

3. What is cash flow?

4. What is the purpose of budgeting?

5. What is a management plan?

CHAPTER 5
Maintaining Your Business

CHAPTER OBJECTIVES

After completing this chapter, you should be able to:

- Describe basic strategies for business communications, and explain how advertising and marketing are circumscribed by consumer protection laws and by rule 8.

- Understand how to charge fees in compliance with rule 5.

- Be aware of the various employment laws, such as the *Employment Standards Act* and the Ontario *Human Rights Code*, and their impact on your hiring and employment practices.

- Understand a range of client retention strategies.

ADVERTISING AND BUSINESS COMMUNICATIONS

Advertising Strategies

Advertising refers to conduct calculated to draw attention to a product or a business in order to encourage sales, generally through paid announcements in various media. All advertising by paralegals must not only be consistent with consumer protection laws, but must comply with rule 2, rule 8.02, and guideline 19.

In order to attract new clients and keep your business running, you will need to use advertising effectively. This will involve determining what form or forms of advertising is or are the most appropriate (based on your client and market profiles), what your advertising budget is, and what message you wish to convey.

Your advertising budget will dictate which media options are available to you to a large degree. In theory, newspapers allow you to reach a wide audience relatively inexpensively, but there is no guarantee your ad will be seen since newspapers are not usually read cover-to-cover. While advertising in a magazine is more expensive, your ad is more likely to be read. Radio spots can be effective and affordable, but must be repeated often. Using electronic media and maintaining a website are two important advertising methods today. Although sending out bulk emails is not effective (due to the overabundance of "spam" mail and increasingly efficient filtering

advertising
efforts to draw attention to a product or a business in order to encourage sales, generally through paid announcements in various media

systems), the strategic use of comments and postings on search engines such as Google and social networking sites is an inexpensive way to help raise your profile.

The media you choose for advertising will depend partly on the type of legal services you are offering and on your targeted client base. For example, if your focus is elder law and your client base consists predominantly of senior citizens, Internet advertising may be less effective than print or radio advertising. Paralegals seeking to represent clients in criminal matters or provincial offences might consider advertising near courthouses.

Paralegals must be diligent in assessing all of their advertising in order to ensure compliance with consumer protection law—such as the *Consumer Protection Act* in Ontario—and rule 8.02. Advertisements must not include deceptive or misleading statements, and must not omit any important information—for example, information regarding hidden fees and surcharges. A technique known as bait and switch, whereby one product or service is advertised to lure customers in and is then replaced with another product or service, is also prohibited. Finally, in order to avoid lawsuits, paralegals must avoid making slanderous or libellous remarks against competitors in their advertisements, and must adhere to copyright and trademark laws.

Determining the message your ads will convey is an important decision. The claims you make should be realistic and credible. Choosing a single, consistent message that is easily understood and concise is often the best approach. A useful step in deciding where and how to allocate advertising funds is by testing what messages work. Researching the market and determining what competitors do and say in their advertising, and what works for them, will provide valuable insights. It may be worthwhile to obtain professional assistance.

Marketing

marketing
a broader concept than advertising that focuses on branding, such as with use of letterhead, business cards, and logos (rule 8.03)

Maintaining a business inevitably involves marketing. **Marketing** is a broader concept than advertising; it includes advertising, distribution, and selling, and involves disciplines as diverse as psychology, sociology, and economics. All interactions with clients and potential clients have an element of marketing. When you are providing services well, you are making a favourable impression and selling your business.

To develop and assess marketing—that is, to generate and refine ideas about how to promote your services—you can conduct market research. Information may be gathered through the use of surveys or client evaluations, and/or research may be conducted either by the business or by third-party professionals. For example, you might provide a comments box in your waiting area, or give clients whose business is concluded an evaluation form asking them for feedback; you might ask about their level of satisfaction and any suggestions for improvement. It is preferable that your clients bring their complaints to you, rather than to other potential clients or the Law Society.

strategic planning
the process of assessing the current business situation and the environment to determine whether it is changing, and revising the business plans to reflect the findings

A marketing strategy is an important part of a business's overall business plan. **Strategic planning** refers to a process that takes place annually in many organizations. Key players within the business assess the current business situation and the environment and determine whether it is changing. This is a time when you can reflect on new trends and opportunities in order to take advantage of them and avoid any negative consequences, such as loss of client base. Your business plan can be fine-tuned (or even altered dramatically) to respond to changes as they unfold. Stepping back from day-to-day operational concerns and putting your mind to the bigger picture and future opportunities is key to the success of your business.

Business Communications

Still broader than the concept of marketing is **business communication**, which encompasses marketing, customer relations, branding, community engagement, advertising, public relations, and employee management. Business communication includes internal communication between employees as well as external communication with clients or the public.

The expanding range of telecommunications technologies has broadened the scope of communications available to businesses. While communicating in person, and through print, radio, and television media remains important, businesses increasingly communicate using email, websites, and online social networking media.

Because external communication shapes your business's brand and public image, controlling this type of communication is critical. Damage done to your business's public image is difficult to repair, and having policies in place regarding who may speak for the enterprise—particularly to the media—is sound practice. Your business may be responsible for communications made on its behalf by anyone acting as its agent, whether the person is an employee, a spokesperson, or even someone who only *seems* to be a spokesperson, such as a relative. Liability can include civil damages, regulatory or statutory liability, as well as accountability to the LSUC.

business communication communication for the purpose of carrying out business activities; includes marketing, customer relations, branding, community engagement, advertising, public relations, and employee management

Rules 2.01 and 8

In addition to restrictions on advertising that apply to all businesses, lawyers and paralegals must know and observe the restrictions imposed by the LSUC.

Rule 2.01 requires paralegals to conduct themselves in a manner that maintains the integrity of the paralegal profession. This obligation is extremely broad, and allows the LSUC to revoke licences for a wide range of conduct that it deems inappropriate. Because of its visibility, advertising may be given a particularly high level of scrutiny by the LSUC.

Rule 8 deals with issues related to practice management, including general obligations, advertising, insurance, firm names, letterhead, and signs. Under rule 8.02, paralegals are required to make legal services available to the public in an efficient and convenient way, and in doing so may not use means

(a) that are false or misleading;

(b) that amount to coercion, duress, or harassment;

(c) that take advantage of a person who is vulnerable or who has suffered a traumatic experience and has not yet had a chance to recover (a practice known as "ambulance chasing");

(d) that are intended to influence a person who has retained another paralegal or lawyer for a particular matter to change his or her representative for that matter, unless the change is initiated by the person or the other representative (a practice known as "poaching"); or

(e) that otherwise bring the paralegal profession or the administration of justice into disrepute.

The last rule above means that the LSUC can sanction paralegals for conduct it deems to be distasteful even if they did not breach any particular rule in their advertising practices; in other words, paralegals must comply not only with the "letter" of the rules but with their "spirit." Paralegals are also prohibited from advertising services that are beyond the permitted scope of practice for paralegals, such as divorce (rule 8.02(3)).

Rule 8.03 addresses marketing, and provides that the term "marketing" includes advertisements and other similar communications in various media as well as firm names (including trade names), letterhead, business cards, and logos. Paralegals may market legal services if the marketing

(a) is demonstrably true, accurate, and verifiable;

(b) is neither misleading, confusing, or deceptive, nor likely to mislead, confuse, or deceive; and

(c) is in the best interests of the public and is consistent with a high standard of professionalism.

This rule also addresses the advertising of fees, and provides that fees may be advertised if

(a) the advertising is reasonably precise as to the services offered for each fee quoted;

(b) the advertising states whether other amounts, such as disbursements and taxes, will be charged in addition to the fee; and

(c) the paralegal adheres to the advertised fee.

Like rule 8.02, the limits imposed by rule 8.03 are broadly framed—for example, that paralegals may only use marketing that is "true, accurate, and verifiable," that is not "misleading," and that is "consistent with a high standard of professionalism." In cases where you are unsure whether or not the LSUC would approve of a particular advertising, marketing, or fees strategy, you may wish to err on the side of caution. The statements in the Rules and the Guidelines are meant to complement—not serve as substitutes for—paralegals' professional judgment.

LETTERHEAD AND SIGNS

The limits on marketing set out in rule 8.03 also apply to the way in which paralegals may identify themselves on signs, letterhead, business cards, and logos—that is, any information that these items contain must be true, accurate, verifiable, and so on. For example, the letterhead of a paralegal sole proprietor should not say "and partners," and a professional corporation must identify itself as such.

Letterheads and signs should not be profane or glib. Certain kinds of catchy and comedic slogans, signs, and logos would not be in keeping with the high standard of professionalism required by the Rules.

SETTING FEES

For paralegals in Ontario, determining what fees to charge for their services is both a business management and a regulatory compliance issue. In setting appropriate fees, paralegals must respond to market demands as well as observe the limitations imposed by the LSUC.

Business Considerations—Fees

In general, paralegal entrepreneurs must set their fees at a level where they can, by working a reasonable amount of hours, cover their costs and earn a profit. Setting fees is a matter of individual strategy on the part of a business, and while conventional economic wisdom suggests that businesses should market their services at a price level that is similar to that of their competitors, there are a number of things you should keep in mind when setting fees.

A good preliminary strategy is determining what "cost-based prices" would be. These are fees that reflect what it costs your business to stay in business (Dern 1991). You should periodically assess and reassess the costs you incur in the course of providing your services to determine the total cost of operating your business. Among the expenditures you should consider are overhead, payroll, and materials; these costs are often underestimated. You should also consider office expenses (such as rent, electric bills, postage, telephone and Internet bills, and so on), professional licensing fees, insurance, and any other memberships and/or subscriptions incidental to your business.

Once you have determined a cost-based amount for your services, there is a good deal of psychological subtlety involved in the business practice of setting final fees. Although the lowest prices may attract more clients in certain business areas, where professional services—and legal services in particular—are concerned, clients may not wish to retain a "bargain basement" paralegal. There is also the question of what value a legal services provider's expertise, education, and experience have in the market. You may wish to look into what other comparable organizations or sole proprietors are charging for similar legal services.

Another aspect of setting appropriate fees is managing client expectations. When a client retainer is entered into, you should review the details of the retainer agreement with the client. The fees that the client can expect to pay and when they will be required to pay them should be made very clear, and a schedule of fees should be provided to the client in writing. Keeping existing clients and gaining new ones through referrals depends largely on how well you manage your clients' expectations. For your clients to feel satisfied with the legal services they are receiving from you, the financial arrangements must be completely transparent.

Fee collection is a common problem faced by practitioners. It is important to ensure that your retainer is replenished as needed, and that you do not invest many hours in a matter only to face non-payment of your invoice. In order to reduce the possibility of misunderstanding or surprise, you should bill your clients regularly and frequently. Your clients may not realize how quickly legal fees can grow to an unanticipated size.

You may wish to accept credit card payments, as this transfers the responsibility for debt collection onto credit card companies. Despite the monthly fees you will pay for this service, it may be a worthwhile investment.

LSUC Rules—Fees

Beyond the general business management considerations discussed above, rule 5 imposes additional constraints on the fees that paralegals may charge.

Rule 5.01(1) provides that all fees and disbursements charged or accepted by paralegals should be fair and reasonable, and must have been disclosed in a timely manner. What is fair and reasonable will depend on factors such as the following (rule 5.01(2)):

(a) the time and effort required and spent;

(b) the difficulty and importance of the matter;

(c) whether special skill or service was required and provided;

(d) the amount involved or the value of the subject matter;

(e) the results obtained;

(f) fees authorized by statute or regulation; and

(g) special circumstances.

Clients must be informed promptly and provided with specific details regarding fees charged. According to rule 5.01(3), paralegals may not accept compensation related to their employment from anyone other than the client, except in cases where they have made full disclosure regarding the arrangement to the client and have obtained the client's consent. This protects clients against a conflict of interest in the event that the interests of the person paying your fee and the interests of your client diverge.

Disbursements are amounts for out-of-pocket expenses relating to a particular file, such as photocopies, postage, long-distance telephone charges, and court filing fees. You may seek reimbursement for these costs from your client, but you must clearly set them apart from the fee portion of your bill in a statement of account (rule 5.01(4)). You may not disburse overhead costs, such as rent.

Paralegals are routinely required to hold money in trust—for example, they hold retainer funds in trust prior to providing their services. Very strict rules apply to funds held in trust, including the fact that they must be kept separate and apart in a trust account. Paralegals may only withdraw funds from their trust accounts in circumstances set out in the Rules—for example, to pay for legal services rendered, and in this case only after the client has been billed.

REFERRAL FEES AND FEE SPLITTING

A referral is the act of suggesting the name of another paralegal or lawyer to a client. According to rule 5.01(13), paralegals may receive a referral fee from another licensee for referring a client if

(a) the referral was not made because of a conflict of interest;

(b) the fee is reasonable and does not increase the total amount of the fee charged to the client; and

(c) the client is informed and consents.

Paralegals sometimes give and receive referrals to and from colleagues who are practising in different areas of law. Many do not charge a fee for such referrals, with the expectation that their colleagues will do the same.

According to rule 5.01(11), paralegals may not split fees. Specifically, they shall not

(a) directly or indirectly share, split, or divide their fees with any person who is not a licensee, including an affiliated entity; or

(b) give any financial or other reward to any person who is not a licensee, including an affiliated entity for the referral of clients or client matters.

The provisions above mean that paralegals may not refer business to other institutions or service providers—such as banks, accountants, or investment advisers—*for a fee*. It does not prohibit them from making referrals where no fee is involved or prohibit non-licensees from working in multi-discipline practices with other kinds of professionals, such as accountants and investment advisers.

CONTINGENCY FEES

Contingency fees are fees that are paid depending on the outcome of a case. Where a case is unsuccessful, no fee is charged. If damages are awarded or successfully negotiated on behalf of your client, you are paid based on a predetermined percentage of the damages amount rather than according to an hourly rate or specified task amount.

contingency fee
a fee paid based on a percentage of the final settlement or judgment, and therefore payable only if the client is successful

Except in criminal or quasi-criminal matters, rule 5 permits paralegals to enter into agreements where their fee is contingent on the successful completion of a matter. An agreement for remuneration by contingency fee must be in writing, and the paralegal must explain to the client the factors that are being used to determine the percentage or other basis of payment, including

- the likelihood of success,

- the nature and complexity of the claim,

- the expense and risk of pursuing it,

- the amount of the expected recovery,

- who is to receive an award of costs, and

- the amount of costs awarded.

Contingency fees may account for part or all of a paralegal's payment for a particular matter.

HIRING EMPLOYEES

Choosing the right employees is critical to the success of your business. You may wish to advertise available positions on the LSUC website or in publications such as the *Ontario Reports*, as well as in newspapers and other online job sites. Most positions are filled by word of mouth, and this is another reason why communicating with colleagues and former classmates is a good idea. When interviewing potential employees, ask questions that will allow you to determine whether particular candidates are competent, trustworthy, and would be a good fit for your organization. Always check references carefully; finding out that a particular individual would not be an asset to your business before—rather than after—you hire him or her will save you time and money later.

Rule 2.03 and the Ontario *Human Rights Code* prohibit discrimination against employees and prospective employees on any of the following grounds: race, ancestry, place of origin, colour, ethnic origin, citizenship, creed, sex, sexual orientation, age, record of offences, marital status, family status, or disability. It is your responsibility to ensure that your recruiting methods do not violate human rights. Examples of unacceptable practices would include advertising a position for a "young graduate" or a "Canadian citizen" and asking candidates in an interview whether they intend to have children within the next few years.

Even if you do not intend to discriminate, practices such as those just described are prohibited and could lead to complaints against you to a human rights commission or the LSUC. Paralegals are responsible for finding out what kinds of accommodations they may be required to make for their employees—for example, accommodating an employee or prospective employee with a physical disability by building a wheelchair ramp or providing special computer equipment or chair. You should consult with the Ontario Human Rights Commission to find out what your specific obligations are in certain situations.

The *Employment Standards Act* governs working conditions for non-union employees and covers such things as minimum wage, overtime, breaks, leaves of absence, and vacation and termination pay. Before you begin hiring employees for your business, you should be familiar with your obligations in these areas; information is available on the Ontario Ministry of Labour website. Regarding the termination of employees, common-law obligations expand on the minimum notice requirements of the Act where there is no employment contract. To protect yourself against wrongful dismissal lawsuits, it is good practice to have written employment contracts that set out specific notice periods.

Before hiring anyone, you must obtain a business number from the Canada Revenue Agency (CRA) and open a payroll deductions account. Deductions for income tax must be made from the employee's pay and held in trust in this account until they are remitted to the CRA. You may also be required to deduct amounts for the Canada Pension Plan and for Employment Insurance.

The *Occupational Health and Safety Act* outlines the rights and duties of various parties in the workplace in order to protect workers from health and safety hazards, while the *Workplace Safety and Insurance Act* governs compensation for workplace injuries and diseases. Your obligations under these statutes may depend on the size of your workforce. You may have taken an employment law course in college, and reviewing your notes before you begin hiring employees will serve you well.

Employee Handbooks

Although employers are under no legal or regulatory obligation to develop an employee handbook, doing so is smart business practice. Employee handbooks detail the organization's mission, policies, and procedures. Because paralegals are responsible for the actions and omissions of their employees, the handbook should reference the Rules, especially those relating to client confidentiality and file storage. They may also include your policies regarding sexual harassment, dress codes, scheduling, parking, smoking, discipline procedures, and other work rules. Procedures for specific work tasks may be outlined in detail.

Employees should be given their handbooks on their first day of work and should be required to sign an acknowledgment that they have understood their contents and obligations. This can prevent misunderstandings and conflicts. Ensure that your employees understand that the handbook is *not* part of their employment contract and that you may amend it at any time.

CLIENT RETENTION STRATEGIES

Advertising and marketing strategies can attract clients to your business, but maintaining relationships with existing clients is often the key to business success. In the legal services business, many client relationships are long term, particularly where the legal services being provided relate to businesses. This is one reason why retaining clients is extremely important. In addition, existing clients can help promote your business, since informal personal referrals remain an important way for legal services providers to attract new clients.

The better your relationships with your clients are, the more likely you are to retain clients and receive referrals. The skills necessary to build better client relationships can be learned and honed, beginning with building trust. To do this, you need to cultivate habits and styles that will convey your credibility, competence, and integrity. The following are five things you can do to help strengthen your relationships with your clients:

- Be Interested

    Make small talk. Talk *with* clients and coworkers rather than *at* them. Try to remember details about their lives. It may be helpful to keep notes attached to client files and to review them briefly before speaking with clients. Set aside time each week to connect with existing clients without an urgent reason to do so. Check in with them to see how they are doing, and what their current goals and interests are. Conveying empathy and "going where the client goes" will help nurture relationships (for more information on creating trust with clients, see Green 2009).

- Dress Appropriately

    The way you present yourself to others is a key aspect of non-verbal communication. Your image and reputation can be shaped by simple habits, such as by wearing clean clothing that fits well and that helps you project confidence. Clients tend to seek legal advice from individuals who look the part—that is, who look more conservative. You should also consider what other messages the way you present yourself might be sending to others. Flashy displays of wealth might be off-putting to some clients, while if you are seeking work from "green" companies you should be mindful of how your attire reflects your attitudes in this regard.

- Be Respectful

   Many people view legal services providers as arrogant and self-involved. Respecting your clients' time will help foster trust, especially when your currency is the billable hour. Don't keep people waiting. Don't be late. Focus your attention entirely on clients when speaking to them. Turn off your telephone, computer, or Blackberry during client meetings. Return client messages promptly; failure to return telephone calls is one of the most common complaints against lawyers and paralegals.

- Showcase Your Knowledge—Appropriately

   If you are working with others, promote the solid team of competent professionals who work with you. If you are a sole practitioner, promote your extensive network of colleagues, your competence, and your confidence. Display your credentials, such as by hanging your diploma and certificates on your office wall.

   Be sensitive to clients' individual needs and tailor your approach. Some may not appreciate small talk (especially if you are charging by the hour), while those who wish to share—even if it's just to vent—will appreciate that you take the time to listen. Make sure to ask your clients what they want to know, and assure them that you have the expertise and experience required to represent them if indeed you do. If you are not competent to handle a matter, be honest with the client and seek assistance, or refer the client to a lawyer or another paralegal. This will enhance rather than detract from your reputation, and will likely generate reciprocal referrals.

- Be Involved

   As your business gets busier, you may be tempted to reduce your involvement in volunteer activities or professional groups. When considering how to balance various demands on your time, keep in mind that the investment in professional and non-profit organizations will pay dividends in the form of high levels of visibility, support networks, and—ultimately—referrals. Establish yourself as an expert among experts.

Building your "you" brand will help you attract new clients, retain existing ones, and will minimize the risk of complaints against you to the LSUC. Your demeanour and conduct should be priorities. Failure to conduct yourself with candour, honesty, and professionalism could lead to the loss of your licence and the end of your business.

CONCLUSION

In their advertising and marketing, paralegals must observe consumer protection laws as well as the rules imposed by the LSUC. The general provision in the Rules that requires paralegals to conduct themselves in a manner that maintains the integrity of the paralegal profession extends to advertising and marketing.

Marketing includes advertisements and other similar communications in various media, as well as firm names (including trade names), letterhead, business cards, and logos. You must ensure that your ads do not omit any important information, and that they do not contain deceptive or misleading statements, or slanderous or libellous remarks against competitors. All marketing must be demonstrably true, accurate, and verifiable, and be consistent with a high standard of professionalism. When advertising fees, the advertising must be reasonably precise as to the services offered for each fee quoted, must not contain hidden fees and surcharges, and the paralegal must adhere to the fee.

The Rules regarding advertising and marketing are broadly framed. Where you are unsure whether or not the LSUC would approve of a particular advertising, marketing, or fees strategy, you may wish to err on the side of caution.

Controlling external communication is critical to preserving your business's public image and reputation. You may be responsible for communications made on behalf of your business by anyone acting as its agent, and liability may include civil damages, regulatory or statutory liability, as well as accountability to the LSUC.

A good starting point when setting fees is to determine a cost-based amount for your services, and then to decide what would be reasonable based on your education, experience, and expertise—and considering what other comparable businesses are charging for similar legal services. You must also observe provisions in the Rules governing fees and disbursements, referral fees, fee splitting, and contingency fees.

Before you begin hiring employees for your business, you should be familiar with your obligations under the *Human Rights Code* and various employment legislation, including the *Employment Standards Act*, the *Occupational Health and Safety Act*, and the *Workplace Safety and Insurance Act*. You must also obtain a business number from the CRA and open a payroll deductions account.

Strong, long-term client relationships built on a foundation of trust are key to the success of your business. In addition to providing repeat business, existing clients can be a source of personal referrals. You can build better client relationships and retain clients by being interested in them as individuals beyond your immediate business relationship with them, by presenting a professional image, by treating them with respect, by displaying your professional knowledge and competence appropriately, and by becoming and staying involved with volunteer activities and professional groups throughout your career.

KEY TERMS

advertising

business communication

contingency fee

marketing

strategic planning

USEFUL URLS

AllBusiness.com, Inc. "Small Business Advertising Basics." http://www.allbusiness.com/marketing/advertising/1417-1.html.

Canada Revenue Agency Business Registration. http://www.businessregistration.gc.ca.

Consumer Protection Act, 2002, S.O. 2002, c. 30, Sch. A.

Ministry of Labour. 2007. "Employment Standards." http://www.labour.gov.on.ca/english/es/index.html.

Ministry of Labour. http://www.labour.gov.on.ca.

Ministry of Labour. WorkSmartOntario. http://www.worksmartontario.gov.on.ca.

REFERENCES

Dern, Daniel P. "The Essential Way to Set Your Fees: A Step-by-Step Guide to Calculating What You Must Charge —Marketing Your Services." 1991. http://findarticles.com/p/articles/mi_m1563/is_n10_v9/ai_11407005.

Employment Standards Act, 2000, S.O. 2000, c. 41.

Green, Charles H. "Create Trust, Gain a Client." 2009. http://trustedadvisor.com/cgreen.articles/27/Create-Trust-Gain-a-Client.

Law Society of Upper Canada (LSUC). "Paralegal Professional Conduct Guidelines." Toronto: LSUC, 2008. http://www.lsuc.on.ca/paralegals/a/paralegal-professional-conduct-guidelines.

Law Society of Upper Canada (LSUC). "Paralegal Rules of Conduct." Toronto: LSUC, 2007, as amended. http://www.lsuc.on.ca/paralegals/a/paralegal-rules-of-conduct.

Occupational Health and Safety Act, R.S.O. 1990, c. O.1.

Workplace Safety and Insurance Act, 1997, S.O. 1997, c. 16, Sch. A.

REVIEW QUESTIONS

1. What is advertising?

2. What is marketing?

3. What is strategic planning?

4. What areas and issues does rule 8 regulate?

5. What should paralegals consider when setting fees?

PART II

Professional Practice and Compliance Issues

CHAPTER 6

Practice Management

CHAPTER OBJECTIVES

After completing this chapter, you should be able to:

- Understand what is meant by professional responsibility for legal services providers in Ontario as set out in rule 8.01(1).

- Understand what is required from paralegals in terms of financial responsibility pursuant to rule 8.01(2).

- Understand the scope of paralegals' supervisory responsibility under rule 8.01(3).

- Understand when and how it is appropriate for paralegals to delegate duties under rule 8.01(4).

- Strategically determine effective, efficient, and ethical ways to delegate tasks to employees.

PROFESSIONAL RESPONSIBILITY

Rule 8.01 requires paralegals to assume professional responsibility for all business with which they are entrusted. This means that they are responsible for everything that happens in their practice, including the actions of their staff. **Professional responsibility** refers to paralegals' obligations to observe the rules and **ethics** of the paralegal profession as set out in the *Law Society Act* and the Rules.

FINANCIAL RESPONSIBILITY

Rule 8.01(2) requires paralegals to meet the financial obligations incurred in the course of their practice on behalf of clients "promptly." The exception is where a paralegal has indicated clearly in writing to the person to whom the debt is owed that it is *not* to be the paralegal's personal obligation.

The requirement to deal with financial obligations "promptly" means that money owed should be paid without undue delay. While delay is unavoidable in some cases, paralegals must not cause or contribute to the delay.

professional responsibility
refers to paralegals' obligations to observe the rules and ethics of the paralegal profession as determined by the LSUC

ethics
a branch of philosophy that seeks to address questions about morality; a codified set of moral rules specific to the performace of professional obligations

By-law 9 and rule 3.07 govern related issues of financial transactions and records, and client property, respectively; guideline 10 provides interpretative advice regarding the interaction of these rules.

Paralegals should take their financial obligations very seriously. Because paralegal regulation is relatively new to the LSUC, it is difficult to know exactly how the Rules will be interpreted and applied. Examining the Guidelines, as well as the interpretation of the Rules applying to lawyers (which are similar to the Paralegal Rules), may be useful. The LSUC has responded harshly in the past to financial wrongdoing on the part of lawyers, and paralegals should be careful and detail oriented with respect to their financial obligations—or will very likely face severe professional consequences from the Law Society.

BOOKS AND RECORDS—BY-LAW 9

By-law 9 outlines paralegals' accounting obligations; you must document all of your financial transactions in various ways. Section 18 requires you to keep detailed records of all financial transactions relating to all money and other property received and disbursed in connection with your professional business. You should familiarize yourself with the contents of By-law 9 and review the LSUC's Paralegal Bookkeeping Guide for more information. You may require the assistance of a bookkeeper or accountant in order to ensure that you are in compliance.

Client Funds—Trust Accounting

According to s. 7 of By-law 9, paralegals have special obligations when handling client funds. Client funds are money that belongs to the client, not to you. Most commonly, you will hold client funds in trust if your client pays you a financial retainer in advance of work and billing for a matter; until you complete the work and bill your client, this money belongs to your client and must be held in trust. You might also hold client funds in trust to facilitate payment of a settlement or a purchase and sale between your client and someone else.

trust account
a separate account that paralegals must maintain to keep client funds held in trust

Trust money must be kept separate and apart from your other business accounts in a separate **trust account**. Although you may have more than one trust account, you will usually have just one in which you hold client funds for numerous clients. You must maintain scrupulous records of any transactions involving your trust account(s), keeping track of how much money belongs to each client and leaving an accounting trail of all monies transferred between the trust account and your own account that is easy to follow. By-law 9, s. 9 outlines your specific obligations.

Trust accounts must be controlled by the paralegal who holds the monies in trust. You are ultimately responsible for any inappropriate withdrawal of client trust funds, and access to the trust account by employees should be restricted. Never sign blank trust cheques or allow others to access blank trust account cheques or electronic banking. It is preferable if signing authority is granted only to other licensees.

Cash Transactions

Paralegals must be very careful when accepting cash from clients. You may not receive more than $7,500 in cash for any client file (By-law 9, s. 4(1)). This restriction aims to prevent money laundering and payment with the proceeds of crime. If a client does not have a chequing account, ask for payment by money order or cashier's cheque.

SUPERVISORY RESPONSIBILITY

Professionalism requires accountability and acceptance of responsibility. "Passing the buck" is *not* professional; **professionals** do not try to fault subordinates or others for their own mistakes. Rule 8 effectively codifies Harry Truman's famous statement "the buck stops here" with reference to paralegals and their work. Rule 8.01(3) provides that paralegals must directly supervise staff and assistants to whom tasks and functions are delegated. This means that, not only may you not blame your employees for your mistakes, you must also take responsibility for mistakes that *they* make, because you are responsible for supervising them.

For the purposes of liability both with reference to LSUC disciplinary proceedings and civil proceedings that may be brought by clients for professional negligence, rule 8.01(3) means that *it is no defence* for a paralegal to blame mistakes or omissions on staff. The public policy behind this rule is to protect the public from untrained or irresponsible people providing legal services. When unlicensed staff work for you, it is your licence on the line.

The obligation to supervise requires that you structure your practice in such a way that you can monitor the work of your staff to ensure that it is done correctly, promptly, and effectively. This may mean that you approve all correspondence and court documents before these leave your office. You should hold regular meetings to answer any questions that staff may have and to receive updates on ongoing matters.

professional
a member of a vocation founded upon specialized education and training and subject to standards of competence and ethics

Delegation

While you are responsible for supervising your employees, you are not required to do everything yourself. As your business grows, you will need to **delegate**—that is, assign tasks to others—in a manner that is effective and that allows you to properly oversee the work of others.

Delegating may not come naturally to many entrepreneurs, but appropriate delegation of tasks is critical to the success of many small businesses. Appropriate delegation of work and authority may also boost morale; staff are often more likely to work harder and feel more personally invested in the success of a business when they can take initiative. Finally, delegating can allow you to spend more time outside of work and avoid burnout.

Paralegals who work in businesses large enough to sustain employees should delegate enough work and authority to ensure that tasks are completed in a timely fashion. In many areas of practice, the provision of legal services involves a good deal of detailed paperwork, administrative work, and other tasks. Preparing court

delegate
to assign tasks to others

documents can involve many hours of photocopying and assembling. Office administration—including banking and paying bills, and purchasing supplies—involves
many time-consuming tasks. It may be difficult for you to fulfill the professional
duties for which you were trained if you are faced with a mountain of paperwork
and odd jobs to complete, and you may find that it makes more financial sense for
you to delegate such tasks to others.

Guideline 18, regarding the supervision of staff, sets out general advice with
respect to delegation of tasks to support staff, including limits on the type of work
that can be delegated and the degree of supervision required. Paralegals should be
satisfied with respect to the competence of the person to whom they are delegating
tasks—in other words, with the staff member's experience, training, and skills. In
addition, paralegal employers must ensure that they hire and train staff properly.
This includes obtaining information about potential employees to assess their competence and trustworthiness.

Any unlicensed employees to whom tasks are delegated must clearly identify
themselves as such in all written and verbal communications.

Your staff must be aware of the following (guideline 18):

- the types of tasks that will and will not be delegated;

- what sort of conduct is and is not appropriate with respect to courtesy and
professionalism;

- the definitions of discrimination and harassment, and the fact that such
conduct is prohibited;

- the definition and scope of the duty to maintain client confidentiality, and
methods to ensure that confidentiality is not breached;

- the definition and scope of what might constitute a conflict of interest, and
how to use the conflict-checking system;

- how to handle client property, including money and other items, properly;
and

- how to keep records properly.

Guideline 18 refers to By-law 7.1 and rules 8.01(1), (3), and (5). Both By-law
7.1 and rule 8.01 make clear that there are tasks that *cannot* be properly delegated
to support staff. According to By-law 7.1, support staff may not give legal advice,
conduct negotiations, sign important correspondence, or forward to a client documents that have not been reviewed by the supervising paralegal. Rule 8.01(4) pro-
hibits non-licensee staff from providing legal services, being held out as licensees,
or performing any of the duties that only paralegals may perform or doing things
that paralegals themselves may not do.

Although paralegals may delegate certain tasks, they remain ultimately responsible for ensuring that those tasks are completed properly. To enable paralegals to
meet this responsibility, By-law 7.1(1) provides that paralegals retain effective control over any non-licensee's provision of services. "Effective control" means that the
licensee may, without the agreement of the non-licensee, take any action necessary
to ensure that the licensee complies with the *Law Society Act*; the by-laws; and the
Society's Rules, Guidelines, and policies (By-law 7.1, s. 1(2)). Paralegals must have

a direct relationship with each client, meaning that the client retains the paralegal and that support staff are not parties to the retainer agreement. Rule 8.01 restates the requirement that paralegals assume complete professional responsibility for all business entrusted to them.

Licensed paralegals may wish to "team up" with professionals from other disciplines, such as accountants and tax consultants, to serve a wider range of client needs. By-law 7, s. 16 allows for such partnerships to support or supplement the provision of legal services only where the business is operated as a **multi-discipline partnership**. All multi-discipline partnerships must obtain approval from the LSUC.

Section 16 also sets limits on the delegation of tasks among professionals working in multi-discipline partnerships. Each professional within such a partnership may only provide the services for which he or she has been trained and is licensed. The licensee partners—paralegals and lawyers—are responsible for the actions of the non-licensee partners and must ensure that professional liability insurance is obtained. You remain accountable to the LSUC for the work of the other professionals with whom you practise.

Even when the following are carried out by employees, By-law 7.1 provides that you are responsible for

- all services rendered,

- all communications made, and

- all materials prepared

on behalf of your business.

Strategically Delegating Duties

Using various outsourced services and entering into contracts with other businesses can allow sole practitioners to enhance their business success. You might consider using answering services, cleaning services, or occasional information support services to make your business run more smoothly. You might also consider delegating certain tasks to professionals who are more highly skilled in certain circumstances— for example, contracting with a lawyer or obtaining legal research from an outside source in a relatively complex case.

Time management is an important part of the ongoing business planning process. This includes scheduling appointments, diarizing due dates, and setting aside time to prepare documents and to complete other tasks. You should document how your time is spent for billing purposes as well as to assess efficiency, noting how much time was spent on client work (billable time) and how much was spent on administrative tasks (non-billable time). If delegating administrative tasks to others will allow you more billable time, this will improve your profitability.

To delegate tasks effectively, you should do the following:

- Determine what work should be delegated.

- Give clear instructions—be clear and precise about employees' responsibilities, the results you want, and any specific methods required to complete the tasks.

- Have a system in place to review employees' work.

multi-discipline partnership
a partnership of licensees and other professionals, such as accountants and tax consultants, through which paralegals can provide their clients with non-legal professional services that support the provision of legal services

- Be specific in explaining what types of decisions employees have the authority to make in the course of performing their tasks, and make clear that they should check with the supervising paralegal before stepping outside of that authority.

- Make sure that employees are aware that they should ask questions or request assistance if they are uncertain of what to do.

- Ensure that employees understand what has been assigned to them. It may be useful to have them repeat their assignments back to you in their own words.

Although you are ultimately responsible to clients and the public for all work you delegate, employees will often perform better if they are made to *feel* they are responsible, and if they feel a sense of ownership and accomplishment with regard to their work. Training is an investment—helping your employees grow professionally will pay off in the long term as they are able to undertake more complex tasks.

CONCLUSION

As a professional, you are responsible for your own actions in your practice as well as for the actions of your staff. Ultimately, you assume professional responsibility for all business with which you are entrusted.

You should take all financial obligations incurred in the course of your practice very seriously, meeting all such obligations promptly unless you have indicated clearly in writing to the person to whom the debt is owed that it is not to be your personal obligation.

As a professional, you must be accountable. Because you are responsible for supervising your employees, you must assume responsibility for any mistakes that they make. With respect to liability with reference to LSUC disciplinary proceedings and civil proceedings, it is no defence to blame mistakes or omissions on staff.

As your businesses grows, you will need to delegate work to others. This can allow you to spend more time fulfilling the professional duties for which you were trained and can help you avoid burnout by allowing you to spend more time outside of work. For your employees, delegation of work and authority may boost morale; staff will feel more personally invested in the success of a business if they are able to take initiative. The Guidelines explain what kind of work can be delegated and the degree of supervision required. Certain tasks cannot be properly delegated to staff, as described in the Rules.

You must ensure that you hire and train all staff properly, and that you are satisfied with respect to the experience, training, and skills of the person to whom you are delegating tasks. All unlicensed employees to whom tasks are delegated must clearly identify themselves as such in all written and verbal communications.

Paralegals may team up with professionals from other disciplines, such as accountants and tax consultants, in multi-discipline partnerships in order to serve a wider range of client needs. All multi-discipline partnerships must obtain approval from the LSUC. Each professional in such a partnership may only provide to clients the services for which he or she has been trained and is licensed; paralegals remain accountable to the LSUC for the work of the other professionals with whom they practise.

Training your employees is an investment. By helping them grow professionally, you will benefit from the new skills they acquire.

KEY TERMS

delegate

ethics

multi-discipline partnership

professional

professional responsibility

trust account

USEFUL URLS

Law Society of Upper Canada (LSUC). 2008. "Paralegal Bookkeeping Guide." http://rc.lsuc.on.ca/jsp/bookkeepingGuide/paralegal.jsp.

Yoskovitz, Ben. 2006. "The Secret to Successfully Delegating Work in 6 Steps." http://www.instigatorblog.com/the-secret-to-successfully-delegating-work-in-6-steps/2006/09/01.

REFERENCES

Law Society Act. R.S.O. 1990, c. L.8, as amended.

Law Society of Upper Canada (LSUC). "By-Laws." 2005. http://www.lsuc.on.ca/regulation/a/by-laws.

Law Society of Upper Canada (LSUC). "Paralegal Professional Conduct Guidelines." Toronto: LSUC, 2008. http://www.lsuc.on.ca/paralegals/a/paralegal-professional-conduct-guidelines.

Law Society of Upper Canada (LSUC). "Paralegal Rules of Conduct." Toronto: LSUC, 2007, as amended. http://www.lsuc.on.ca/paralegals/a/paralegal-rules-of-conduct.

REVIEW QUESTIONS

1. What is professional responsibility?

2. What is a trust account, and what are the obligations of paralegals with respect to client funds held in trust?

3. What is a paralegal's supervisory responsibility and how does this relate to liability for errors and omissions on the part of staff?

4. Describe some steps a paralegal should take in delegating tasks.

CHAPTER 7

Clients and the Public

CHAPTER OBJECTIVES

After completing this chapter, you should be able to:

- Understand the obligations of paralegals with respect to competence.

- Understand the obligations of paralegals with respect to advising clients.

- Understand the obligations of paralegals with respect to confidentiality.

- Indentify who "clients" are and understand the duties of paralegals to their clients.

- Understand the obligations of paralegals with respect to conflicts of interest.

- Understand how to use technology effectively, and in accordance with the Rules and your professional obligations, in your communications with clients.

- Recognize the requirement in rule 8.04 for errors and omissions insurance, and understand its importance.

- Understand best practices for, and know how to create, a retainer agreement.

DEALING WITH CLIENTS

Unlike customers, who purchase products, clients are purchasers of services—for example, legal services. Rule 3 sets out the duties of paralegals to their clients. You must balance these duties with your duties to the administration of justice and the general public.

Competence

According to rule 3.01(1), paralegals must perform all services undertaken on a client's behalf to the standard of a competent paralegal. A **competent paralegal** is a paralegal who has and applies the relevant skills, attributes, and values appropriate to each matter undertaken on a client's behalf (rule 3.01(4)). These may include—but are not limited to—legal research, analysis, writing and drafting, negotiation, and advocacy.

competent paralegal
a paralegal who has and applies the relevant skills, attributes, and values appropriate to each matter undertaken on a client's behalf (rule 3.01(4))

Rule 3.01(4)(l) states that paralegals must comply with the Rules "in letter and in spirit"—in other words, as a professional you are expected to embrace the Rules to the fullest extent. It is not appropriate to look for loopholes or gaps to exploit.

To be competent, you must be able to properly perform any task that you agree to take on. Part of this involves recognizing the limitations of your training and expertise. You must not attempt to perform tasks that are too complex for you to properly complete or undertake to do things you cannot handle. If you discover in the course of a matter that you do not possess the knowledge or experience necessary for you to continue, you should obtain the client's consent to consult with a lawyer, or refer the file to another paralegal. It is not worth risking your reputation and licence by working on matters that are outside your area or areas of expertise when there are others that you can competently manage on your own.

Advising Clients

Rule 3.02 requires paralegals to be honest and candid when advising clients, and to provide advice only within their permitted scope of practice. For example, paralegals should not provide financial advice, since they are not licensed to do so.

The advice that paralegals may give to clients is also limited by their broader duties to the public and to the administration of justice. You may not knowingly assist in or encourage any dishonesty, fraud, crime, or illegal conduct—for example, you may not advise a client to lie under oath or in a sworn affidavit, or on how to break the law and avoid punishment (rule 3.02(3)).

Paralegals must take reasonable measures to avoid becoming the "tool or dupe" of an unscrupulous client or that client's associates (rule 3.02(4)). For example, do not accept large cash retainers and return the funds by cheque; this is a common form of money laundering. From a practice management perspective, you must be careful about the clients you take on, and you must scrutinize the instructions you are given to satisfy yourself that you are not being used for illegal purposes.

Rule 3.02(5) obligates paralegals to encourage their clients to compromise or settle whenever doing so is possible on a reasonable basis. You must also inform your clients about alternative dispute resolution options—such as mediation, negotiation, or arbitration—and advise them regarding the availability and feasibility of each of these (rule 3.02(6)).

Paralegals should never add fuel to the fire of a conflict for their own purposes—namely, to create more fees. While resolving matters quickly may mean that you make less money on each file, a paralegal business is not only a business for the purpose of maximizing earnings, but a profession with the numerous responsibilities and obligations imposed by the LSUC.

Rule 3.02(7) addresses clients under a disability—that is, clients whose ability to make decisions is impaired because of age, mental disability, or for some other reason. Paralegals should maintain a normal professional relationship with such clients as far as is reasonably possible. However, if a client loses the capacity to manage his or her legal affairs, you must take steps to have a representative appointed for that client.

Paralegals must advise French-speaking clients of their official language rights, including their right to be served by a paralegal who speaks French (rule 3.02(14)). You should consider networking with paralegals who provide services in French so that you can refer clients as necessary.

Confidentiality

Like certain other professionals, such as physicians and social workers, paralegals have a duty to keep client matters confidential, as outlined in rule 3.03. Clients are entitled to trust that paralegals will hold their confidential information in strict confidence. **Confidential information** is any information that paralegals gain in the course of their professional relationship with a client. To ensure confidentiality, paralegals must keep the client's papers and other property out of the sight and reach of those who are not entitled to see them.

The duty of confidentiality continues indefinitely after the paralegal has finished acting for a client. However, paralegals may be required to disclose confidential information in certain situations—for example, when required by law or order of a tribunal (rule 3.03(4)). They may also disclose what confidential information is necessary to defend against allegations of criminal wrongdoing, malpractice, or misconduct (rule 3.03(6)).

Confidentiality, like advising clients, is an area where your duties to your client and your duties to the general public and the administration of justice may conflict. Under rule 3.03(5), paralegals may disclose confidential information relating to a client if they have reasonable grounds to believe that there is an imminent risk of death or serious bodily harm—including serious psychological harm that substantially interferes with health or well-being—to an identifiable person or group, and that disclosing the confidential information is necessary to prevent the death or harm. For example, if a client tells you that he will kill his landlord with the gun he bought last week if the broken furnace isn't fixed and you reasonably believe that he may carry through on this threat, you *may* disclose the threat to the police, though you are not obligated to.

You should note that a paralegal's professional obligation of confidentiality is distinct from the legal doctrine of solicitor–client privilege, whereby certain communications between a lawyer and a client are legally protected from disclosure and are inadmissible in court. This is a broader protection than confidentiality, as confidential communications may be ordered disclosed by a court in certain circumstances. Although the doctrine of privilege generally does not apply to communications between a paralegal and a client, there is case law in which certain communications made by a client to a paralegal were held to be privileged (see, for example, *R. v. McClure*).

> **confidential information**
> any information that paralegals gain in the course of their professional relationship with a client; paralegals have a duty to hold all such information in strict confidence indefinitely and may not disclose it to any other person, unless authorized to do so by the client or required to do so by law (rule 3.03(1))

Conflicts of Interest and Identifying Clients

Paralegals are obligated to act with loyalty to their clients. This means that they must represent the interests of each client exclusively. There are numerous circumstances that may present a **conflict of interest**, defined at rule 3.04(1) as an interest, financial or otherwise, that may negatively affect a paralegal's ability to fulfill his or her professional and ethical obligations to a client. For example, it would be a conflict of interest to act as paralegal to your landlord in drafting a tenancy agreement, because your personal interests might conflict with your client's. Similarly, it might be a conflict of interest to act for a client who is suing your cousin in Small Claims Court. You must avoid conflicts of interest in your dealings with clients. Where this is not possible, you should refer clients to another paralegal or lawyer.

> **conflict of interest**
> an interest, financial or otherwise, that may negatively affect a paralegal's ability to fulfill the professional and ethical obligations owed to a client

A conflict of interest will arise if your loyalty and ability to represent a client's interests are compromised, or even if these *appear* to be compromised. Rules 3.04, 3.05, and 3.06 provide that a paralegal may not

- act against former clients in any matter;

- act against persons involved or associated with a former client in a matter, unless the client's written consent is obtained;

- represent more than one side in a dispute; or

- act in a matter where the paralegal's personal, financial, or other interests are in conflict, or potential conflict, with those of the client.

client
a purchaser of services; includes, but is not limited to, a former client, and a client of the paralegal firm of which the paralegal is a partner or employee, whether or not the paralegal handles the client's work (rule 1.02)

The term **client** has an expansive meaning under the Rules. It includes, but is not limited to, a client of the paralegal firm of which the paralegal is a partner or employee, whether or not the paralegal handles the client's work (rule 1.02). In other words, your partner's clients are your clients, and vice versa. This is an important concept to keep in mind when considering conflicts of interest. If your partner or employee is representing a party to a dispute, you may not represent the opposing party, as this would be a conflict of interest. For the purpose of assessing whether there is a conflict of interest, former clients of your firm are considered clients.

A common question that arises in various situations is: Who is the client? Although it may seem obvious that the client is the person with whom the paralegal (or firm) contracts to provide legal services, identifying who the client is can be difficult. Consider the following:

- An officer, director, or shareholder of a corporation comes into your office. Who will you be representing—the individual or the corporation?

- You are paid by the parent of a young person charged with a minor criminal offence. Whose instructions do you follow?

- You are representing a landlord in a landlord–tenant matter in which the tenant is unrepresented. In the process of negotiating on behalf of your client, the tenant asks you questions about the law. What do you say?

- You are representing two co-accuseds who tell the same story. Later, one co-accused points the finger at the other. What do you do?

It is imperative that you make clear to all involved in a matter who is and who is not a client, particularly in cases where one party to a dispute is unrepresented. To comply with rule 3, you should do the following in the situations described above:

- Where there is a corporation involved, you should clarify the client's identity at your initial meeting. You may represent either the corporation or an individual, such as a shareholder or director, but probably not both. For example, if there is more than one shareholder, the interests of the corporation are not necessarily aligned with the interests of any particular shareholder.

- If you are paid by someone other than the client, make sure that the client is aware of the payment arrangement and consents to it. Ensure that everyone understands that you are representing the client, not the payer—and that you take instructions from the client only.

- If you are negotiating with an unrepresented party, that party must be aware that you are not acting as a mediator or providing assistance to both your client and that party, but that you represent only your client. You should encourage the unrepresented party to seek independent legal advice.

- Often in the course of legal matters, the interests of two or more clients that initially appeared to coincide begin to conflict. In this case, you may not be able to represent either client, because the confidential information you have gathered creates a conflict of interest.

Withdrawal from Representation

Rule 3.08 governs withdrawal from representation, including circumstances where this is optional, mandatory, and prohibited. Unlike other professionals, who may "fire" their clients at will, paralegals may not withdraw their services whenever they wish—particularly when representing clients in criminal and quasi-criminal matters. This is because of the significant consequences that may result for their clients, who may not be able to retain new counsel in time to meet deadlines or attend at court dates.

Even if a client is refusing or unable to pay you, once you have been retained there are limits on your ability to withdraw. You may be required to go to court to show that your client's case will not be prejudiced if you withdraw from representation. If no prejudice to your client will result, you may withdraw in the circumstances set out in rule 3.08. Generally, you may withdraw if you have lost confidence in your client's ability to inform you of the facts in a forthright and honest manner, or if your client has lost confidence in you for any reason. You may also usually withdraw if your client is failing to pay your fees. You must provide notice of your intention to withdraw, and provide the client with a reasonable opportunity to pay. You may not use the threat of withdrawal to push your client to make a difficult decision—for example, to settle.

Rule 3.08 requires you to withdraw if your client is demanding that you conduct yourself in violation of the Rules, or illegally, or if your client is taking a position solely for the purpose of harassing someone.

Technology and Client Communications

Advances in communications technology have revolutionized the way in which legal services are provided today. Legal research, administration, the drafting of documents, and even filings can now be done electronically, and communications with clients are often carried out online. Regardless of whether you are communicating by paper, email, over the telephone, or in person, you are held to the same standards of professionalism and competence outlined in rules 2 and 3. Adopting an informal tone in email, "blogging" about confidential client information, or discussing confidential matters in social networking forums are all examples of ways that para-legals might breach their professional obligations through misuse of technology. You should be as formal in your electronic communications as you are when using more traditional forms of written communication, and should retain copies of all electronic communications with client files.

You are responsible for ensuring the confidentiality of client information in electronic form. To this end, you may need to use firewalls, antivirus software, and passwords to ensure that third parties cannot access client information. You should also include a statement on emails indicating that they are intended to be confidential. Posting confidential client information online, whether on purpose or inadvertently, can give rise to complaints against you to the LSUC, and to lawsuits for negligence and defamation.

The following suggestions will help you foster solid client relationships, and will allow you and your clients to derive the greatest benefit from your use of technology:

- Personalize Voice Mail

    Personalize voice mail messages and avoid using them if possible. Clients telephone offices to speak with a person and will be unhappy to receive an automated response. If voice mail is necessary, your outgoing message should be re-recorded frequently with date and time statements, and should include a commitment to return calls within a certain timeframe.

- Set Up Systems Mindfully

    Position computers, faxes, and other communications technologies in such a way as to ensure ease of access and protect confidentiality. Make sure that systems are properly maintained, and employ or contract out appropriate technical support services. Ensure that your software systems are secure, and that they are shielded from viruses and security breaches. Do not share email or other identifying information about clients without their consent.

- Be Reachable and Communicate Sensibly

    Technology should make your life easier, and should make it easier for your clients to communicate with you. Clients should be able to access your direct voice mail or email quickly, and you should pick up or read messages promptly to determine their urgency. Clients should only be sent relevant communications. If you spam your clients with irrelevant information, they are more likely to miss important communications when you do send these. Remember that rule 2 requires that you act with courtesy and civility, and prohibits all forms of harassment.

- Draw the Line

    Communication technologies allow us to work at any time, from almost anywhere. However, just because we *can* respond to client communications instantly does not mean that we should. A considered response sent after an appropriate time period will serve the client's interests and help you maintain a healthy work schedule.

For more information regarding the use of technology in your practice, consult the technology section of the LSUC's Practice Management Guidelines

ERRORS AND OMISSIONS INSURANCE

Rule 8.04 mandates that all paralegals practising in Ontario must obtain and maintain adequate **errors and omissions insurance** (also called professional liability insurance). The Law Society will determine what is "adequate" from time to time. Paralegals are required to work cooperatively with their insurers to make sure that claims against them are resolved efficiently, and are personally responsible for paying any amount of liability over that covered by their insurance.

The requirement that paralegals carry errors and omissions insurance protects clients as well as paralegals. It assures clients that they will be compensated for any successful negligence actions against their paralegals, and it assures paralegals that they will not risk losing personal assets to pay any judgments made against them. Generally, the insurer will pay the amount of any damages award made against the insured *and* the costs of defending the claim. This is important because, even in the case of groundless claims, legal fees can be very costly.

errors and omissions insurance
the insurance that covers an individual licensee in the event that a client is successful in suing for professional negligence; also called professional liability insurance

RETAINER AGREEMENTS

A **retainer agreement** is a contract between two parties through which one pays to reserve the other's time and secures the performance of professional services. Where the retainer is for legal services, the paralegal or lawyer who is retained is obligated to act for the client. Consequently, he or she is prevented from acting for another party in the same dispute without the client's consent or for an opposing party in another matter at a later date.

From a practice management perspective, a retainer agreement serves several important functions:

retainer agreement
a contract between the client and the paralegal that confirms that the paralegal has been hired to provide legal services to the client, and defines the parameters of the relationship

- It is a tool for explaining and clarifying the paralegal's professional obligations. You may wish to inform your client, for example, that court procedures may be delayed due to factors beyond your control. Clearly define who your client is, and outline the scope of the retainer—what services you will and will not provide. This will reduce the risk of misunderstanding.

- It is a method for managing client expectations. Being upfront and transparent about the cost of legal fees reduces the likelihood of disputes regarding bills and increases the likelihood that you will collect fees for the services you provide. For example, you may wish to inform your client in the agreement that he or she will be charged for all telephone calls, emails, and messages.

- It can provide a defence in the event of a lawsuit or a complaint. If the details of the retainer agreement are explicit, fair, and clear, this may protect you from potential lawsuits by the client and/or complaints to the Law

Society should a misunderstanding arise on any of the issues described above.

Retainer agreements should be made in writing at the beginning of the paralegal–client relationship. They should ideally be signed by the client before you agree to be retained and should outline the terms of the relationship between you and the client. They should include the following:

- a clear statement of the names and other identifying information about the paralegal (or firm) and client;

- a statement regarding the extent of the paralegal's licence (for example, that the paralegal is a paralegal licensed by the LSUC to practise in Ontario);

- a statement indicating that the client and paralegal have reviewed the paralegal's basic ethical obligations;

- a description of the scope of representation (for example, "for legal advice pertaining to an immigration application" or "for a consultation");

- a statement that the paralegal cannot guarantee any particular outcome with regard to the matter;

- a listing of fees and the manner in which they will be billed;

- a listing of other matters that may be billed, such as mileage, travel time, and other costs (for example, courier fees and court filing disbursements);

- a description of what (if any) financial retainer will be paid in advance of the work to be done, and how billings will be deducted from the retainer;

- a statement regarding dispute resolution (for example, it may be useful for the parties to agree to mediate any disputes respecting the bill or the services before initiating litigation rather than to take these matters directly to court); and

- general contract terms, including a statement of governing law, which makes clear that any disputes with regard to the retainer or fees are to be litigated in Ontario.

With regard to fees, if billings are done by hourly rate, then the retainer agreement should set out the hourly rates; if they are done on a contingency fee basis, the details of these arrangements should be set out. If more than one person works on the file (for example, an employee to whom work is delegated in addition to the paralegal), the hourly rates of all relevant persons should be specified. You may also include a statement to the effect that you will only bill for time reasonably and necessarily incurred, and note any maximum amounts or limits to be charged for certain tasks, if you have agreed to any. Finally, you should outline how often the client will be billed and how the bills should be paid.

retainer
the advance payment made by a client, usually at the time that the retainer agreement is signed, which is deposited in the paralegal's trust account

The term **retainer** is used to describe the advance payment made by a client, which is deposited in the paralegal's trust account. A financial retainer is usually paid at the time that the retainer agreement is signed. As the paralegal bills the client for legal services rendered, the amount billed may be withdrawn from the trust account and deposited into the general account. The paralegal may request that the client replenish the retainer from time to time, as it is billed out. Insisting on a financial retainer before work is done is a prudent business practice, as collecting client fees after the fact can be difficult.

CONCLUSION

Clients are purchasers of services—for example, legal services. You must perform all services undertaken on behalf of your clients to the standard of a competent paralegal, and should not undertake to do things that you cannot handle.

When advising clients, you must be honest and candid, and provide advice only within your permitted scope of practice. In addition, you may not knowingly assist in or encourage any dishonesty, fraud, crime, or illegal conduct when providing advice, and must take reasonable measures to avoid becoming the "tool or dupe" of an unscrupulous client or that client's associates.

When dealing with clients under a disability, you should maintain a normal professional relationship as far as is reasonably possible. If a client loses the capacity to manage his or her legal affairs, you must take steps to have a representative appointed for that client. Whenever possible on a reasonable basis, you must encourage your clients to compromise or settle. You should never draw out a matter for the purpose of creating more fees.

Identifying who the client is can be difficult. It is imperative that you make clear to all involved in a matter who is and who is not a client, particularly in cases where one party to a dispute is unrepresented. You must avoid conflicts of interest in your dealings with clients and, where this is not possible, refer clients to another paralegal or lawyer.

You must hold all information that you gain in the course of your professional relationships with clients in strict confidence indefinitely, except if you are required by law or by order of a tribunal to disclose such information. You may also disclose confidential information if doing so is necessary in order for you to defend yourself against allegations of criminal wrongdoing, malpractice, or misconduct; and if you have reasonable grounds to believe that there is an imminent risk of death or serious bodily harm to an identifiable person or group and that disclosing the information is necessary to prevent the death or harm.

Regardless of whether you are communicating by paper, email, over the telephone, or in person, you are held to the same standards of professionalism and competence outlined in rules 2 and 3. You should be as formal in your electronic communications as you are when using more traditional forms of written communication, and should take all necessary steps to ensure the confidentiality of client information in electronic form.

To foster solid client relationships and to allow you and your clients to derive the greatest benefit from your use of technology, you should personalize voice mail messages and avoid using them if possible; set up and maintain systems mindfully; make sure that clients are able to access your direct voice mail or email quickly, and that you pick up or read messages promptly; and ensure that you know where to draw the line in your use of technology.

Retainer agreements should be made in writing at the beginning of the paralegal–client relationship. They should outline the terms of the relationship between you and the client, and should include—among other things—a description of the scope of representation, a statement indicating that you and the client have reviewed your ethical obligations, a listing of fees and the manner in which they will be billed, a description of what (if any) financial retainer will be paid in advance of the work to be done, and a statement regarding dispute resolution.

KEY TERMS

client

competent paralegal

confidential information

conflict of interest

errors and omissions insurance

retainer

retainer agreement

USEFUL URLS

Law Society of British Columbia. 2009. Sample Retainer Agreement. http://www.lawsociety.bc.ca/practice_support/articles/ retainer-general_short.html.

Law Society of Upper Canada (LSUC). 2009. "Practice Management Guidelines." http://rc.lsuc.on.ca/pdf/pmg/pmg.pdf.

Solove, Daniel J. *The Future of Reputation: Gossip, Rumor, and Privacy on the Internet.* New Haven, CT: Yale University Press, 2007. http://docs.law.gwu.edu/facweb/dsolove/Future-of-Reputation/text.htm.

Wertz, Glenda. 2004. "The Ins and Outs of Errors and Omissions Insurance." *Insurance Journal.* http://www.insurancejournal.com/magazines/ west/2004/07/19/features/44745.htm.

REFERENCES

Law Society of Upper Canada (LSUC). "Paralegal Rules of Conduct." Toronto: LSUC, 2007, as amended. http://www.lsuc.on.ca/paralegals/a/paralegal-rules-of-conduct.

R. v. McClure, [2001] S.C.J. No. 13 (Ont. Master).

REVIEW QUESTIONS

1. Who is a client?

2. To what standard are paralegals required to provide services undertaken on behalf of their clients? Explain the meaning of the standard.

3. Explain the duty of confidentiality.

4. What is a conflict of interest?

5. What must paralegals keep in mind when communicating electronically?

6. Can paralegals share their email lists (that is, the email addresses of their clients and business contacts) with advertisers in exchange for financial compensation?

CHAPTER 8

File Management and Time Management

CHAPTER OBJECTIVES

After completing this chapter, you should be able to:

- Appreciate the importance of client confidentiality.
- Understand how to maintain client confidentiality by using proper systems for file management.
- Describe how to effectively and efficiently use systems and tools, including checklists and ticklers, to manage files.
- Understand how to use and maintain time dockets effectively.
- Plan for effective organization of file contents.
- Understand how to manage clients' property according to rule 3.07.
- Understand how to store active client files.
- Understand how to close and store inactive client files.

CONFIDENTIALITY

The Rules, as well as a long history of legal tradition, provide that effective legal advice requires full and unreserved communication between client and counsel. Confidentiality facilitates this communication. Paralegals must hold all information related to them by clients in the course of their professional relationships in strict confidence. Following the best practices outlined below will assist you in complying with this requirement.

Preserve Privilege If Possible

Although confidentiality and solicitor–client privilege are distinct concepts, there are important links between them. Client information can cease to be confidential if it is ordered into court because it is found *not* to be privileged.

At the time of writing, although it would better serve client interests if communications between clients and paralegals were privileged, it is not clear that they will be. You can increase the likelihood that you, as a paralegal, will be able to claim privilege with regard to client communications by noting a claim to such privilege on documents, including email communications. When requesting information from clients or others, you should note that the request is being made for the purposes of providing legal advice. Similarly, in reply emails or letters, you should indicate that the communication is being made in response to a request for legal advice. You should maintain a professional tone in all communications.

Avoid Inadvertent Disclosure

For most legal services providers, the major pitfall with regard to disclosure of confidential client communications or information is not deliberate disclosure, but inadvertent disclosure. Guideline 8, regarding confidentiality, provides steps to help you protect confidential client information. You should:

- not disclose having been consulted or retained by a particular person unless the nature of the matter requires disclosure;

- not disclose to one client confidential information about another client, and decline any retainer that would require such disclosure;

- avoid indiscreet conversations about your clients' affairs, including with your spouse or family;

- not gossip about client affairs, even when the gossip does not involve naming or otherwise identifying the client;

- not repeat gossip or information about a client's business or affairs that you overhear or that is recounted to you; and

- avoid taking part in or listening to indiscreet "shop talk" between colleagues that may be overheard by third parties.

It is important that you think carefully before engaging in seemingly innocent conversation that may in fact be a breach of confidentiality, especially if you know clients on a personal basis or have common acquaintances—for example, if your client was referred to you by another client.

Office Procedures

Guideline 8 recommends office procedures that can help you protect the confidentiality of clients and avoid conflicts of interest. You should:

- Record identifying information and particulars about every client or potential client. A useful way of doing this is to take basic information before making an appointment to see the client.

- Screen for conflicts of interest at the first contact with a client using the identifying information you recorded. You should do this before you give the client any advice and before the client discloses any confidential information to you.

- Establish a communication policy with each client in which you outline how communications will be conducted. Are electronic communications acceptable? What is the client's preferred contact telephone number? Can messages be left at a home telephone number? Where should letters be sent?

- Set up your office in such a way that client files, file cabinets, and computers cannot be seen and/or accessed by non-employees. Be sure to shred confidential information before discarding it, and ensure appropriate security for off-site storage of files.

- Take steps to protect confidential information obtained and sent in electronic form.

- Train and supervise all staff to ensure they understand their obligations with respect to confidentiality.

- Limit access to confidential information by outside service providers. For example, if business evaluators, accountants, or lawyers are contracted for services on a particular file, they should only be provided with the information they require to complete their tasks.

Once you have office procedures in place, ensure that they are followed consistently, even when things get hectic.

SYSTEMS AND TOOLS FOR MANAGING CLIENT FILES

The LSUC's Practice Management Guidelines were written to help lawyers assess, maintain, and enhance the quality of their services, but the framework they provide for conducting various aspects of legal work will also help paralegals meet their professional obligations and ensure compliance with the Rules.

Professionalism mandates—and the file management section of the Practice Management Guidelines recommends—the creation, collection, and maintenance of the following in managing client files:

- databanks of key information regarding current and former clients, including

  ◇ clients' names, aliases, and former names,

  ◇ the dates files were opened and/or closed,

  ◇ the subject matter of each file;

- information regarding conflicting or adverse parties, including

  ◇ names of persons related to, or associated with, a client or former client, or the names of persons relevant to client or former client matters,

  ◇ cross references to the client or former client file name, file number, and matter reference;

- information regarding billing and accounting;

- information regarding key dates with reference to files, such as a tickler or other time management system.

Every time a client retains your services, a new client file should be opened, even if it contains only the date and time of a consultation. The file should be opened only after a conflict check has been performed and no conflict has been found. Each file should have its own folder.

Various computer software programs can assist you in managing client files, including PCLaw, Amicus Attorney, and LawStream. Although client files are generally kept in hard copy, as more legal business is conducted online it may be appropriate for you to have electronic files in certain situations. Whatever the format of your files, you must keep each file and its contents secure.

For a more comprehensive description and discussion of client file management practices, see Collis and Forget (2007).

Tickler Systems and Checklists

In order to meet your obligations under the Rules—particularly rule 3.01, which requires paralegals to perform all services undertaken on a client's behalf to the standard of a competent paralegal—it is important that you document all work to be done and dates of importance with regard to each client file (see also guideline 6). Failure to take all necessary steps (such as drafting, serving, and filing of documents) or to remember the dates and times of events (such as court dates, meetings, limitation periods, and other deadlines) in relation to a particular matter may cause you to breach your professional obligations and may result in a claim of professional negligence against you.

tickler
a system that is used to provide notice of future obligations and events, such as court dates, meetings, limitation periods, and other deadlines

Two important tools you should employ to manage and meet your obligations are tickler systems and checklists. **Ticklers** will provide you with advance notice of upcoming obligations and events. For example, you will want to be reminded of a deadline in advance of the last day for serving documents so that you have time to prepare them and serve them. You can also use your tickler system to manage other business-related obligations—for example, if utility bills are due on the first day of each month and rent is due on the last day, you can set these as recurring items on your tickler, noted a few days in advance so that those responsible have adequate time to arrange for payment.

checklist
a list of things to be done or steps to be taken in relation to a file or other aspect of business management

A **checklist** is a list of things to be done or steps to be taken in relation to a file or other aspect of business management. Checklists can help you to stay organized, break tasks down into manageable chunks, and meet your professional obligations. They can also serve as a record of the fact that certain tasks were completed, and when. This can be useful in the event that you need to defend yourself against a claim of incompetence or negligence.

You can append a checklist to each client file to identify the steps you must take in relation to the file, such as drafting, serving, and filing of certain documents. Depending on the matter and your type of practice, the contents of your checklists will differ. A checklist for a litigation matter, for example, might contain the following items:

- initial client interview;

- retainer arrangements made, paid, and signed;

- confirm retainer with initial letter stating terms of engagement;

- instruct client regarding what to preserve in relation to the case;

- obtain copies of any statements made by a client;

- obtain copies of any court documents relating to the file;

- obtain copies of basic client documents;

- determine what fact gathering needs to be done; and

- note limitation periods, serving and filing deadlines, and deadlines and obligations with regard to discovery and/or disclosure.

Computer software programs are used increasingly to ensure that deadlines and obligations are met. Many systems—such as the ones mentioned above—provide electronic checklists and tickler systems, which offer advantages over paper-based systems. Electronic systems can be used remotely via the Internet and can synchronize the calendars of various users, and data that is backed up or saved in electronic form can be stored more securely than notes written on paper.

Although they offer advantages, software systems can be quite expensive, and at the outset of your business other programs—or even a paper desk calendar—will likely serve you adequately. You can access free calendars online (such as the ones made available by Google), and less expensive calendar programs are available with basic word-processing and office software. Many legal services professionals use devices such as BlackBerries and iPods to set up their tickler systems and checklists.

Tickler systems for client service obligations and for business management can be kept separately or combined. The advantage of using one system is that you can use a single tool to view all of your obligations on a given date and immediately identify any scheduling conflicts. You may also wish to enter personal obligations into the same system.

Docketing

You will hear the term "docket" or "court docket" used to refer to a list of court cases or other matters scheduled over a particular day or other period of time, and assigned to a specified judge. In the context of practice management, a **time docket** is a record of time spent on billable and non-billable matters that details the work that was done, on what matter, and how long it took to complete.

Billable time is time that is charged to a client on an invoice, so it is important that you document this accurately. Most lawyers and many paralegals choose to charge clients for time spent working on a file, as opposed to other methods such as block fees for completion of specific tasks, or contingency fees. The choice is yours, and you may choose to utilize a combination of methods. However, if you are charging for your time, you must keep track of it!

Non-billable time is time that is not billed to the client, including time spent on things such as professional development and continuing education, marketing, community service work, and business management. Documenting your non-billable time is important because it can help you determine which activities are inefficient or unproductive, and allow you to plan for future budgeting by calculating how much time must be spent on administrative and other business tasks. By monitoring your non-billable time, you may discover that you can operate a more

time docket
a record of time spent on billable and non-billable matters detailing work done, for how long, and on what matter

billable time
time that is charged to a client

non-billable time
time docketed but not billed to a client, such as time spent on professional development, continuing education, marketing, and business management

profitable practice if you delegate such tasks to others, such as an administrative assistant, a process server, a cleaning service, a bookkeeper, or an information technology specialist. Your time is usually better spent focusing on providing legal services for your clients.

Although you will seek to maximize billable time in order to ensure that the amount of money coming into your practice exceeds your expenses, both billable and non-billable time are crucial to the operation of a successful, ethical, and financially viable paralegal practice. In the long term, your practice and your reputation will be greatly enhanced by your ability to make appropriate use of non-billable time.

Software systems designed for use in the legal services industry often have complex docketing systems that allow for electronic record keeping in nuanced ways. Many can provide statistical analysis of time spent in various capacities, which is useful for financial analysis and planning, and in determining appropriate compensation for employees. However, you may also docket by recording time spent on files in spreadsheets or on paper. Whatever method you choose, the key to effective docketing is recording your time consistently and promptly. You should have the docketing software or paper docket on your desktop, and you should docket throughout the business day rather than at the end of it. You will be surprised at how quickly you forget, especially if you are dealing with several matters throughout the day.

ORGANIZING FILE CONTENTS

Ultimately, how you organize your files is a combination of professional judgment and personal preference. What is most important is that you have systems in place, and that files are accessible and organized in a manner that makes them usable. The file management section of the LSUC's Practice Management Guidelines recommends that you employ systems that allow you to

- store and efficiently retrieve information about clients and opposing parties;

- check for any potential conflicts;

- check for limitation periods that may affect the work to be done on a file;

- close, retain, and appropriately dispose of client files;

- review on an ongoing basis and, where necessary, change management systems to keep them effective and up to date;

- identify and place clients' property in safekeeping; and

- comply with the LSUC's bookkeeping and record-keeping requirements.

The file management section also suggests that it is often useful to organize client files into subfiles or subfolders that contain only a certain class or type of document. Depending on the type of file and the nature of the matter, you might have subfiles for:

- communications (documentation of all telephone conversations and their details, any memos regarding client conversations and meetings, and copies of emails sent and received);

- research (including relevant case law, substantive research memoranda, and any investigations that have been done with respect to the file);

- original documents pertaining to the file (for example, a statement of claim in a civil litigation, or forms in an immigration matter);

- the retainer (including the signed retainer agreement as well as receipts for any monies received);

- firm accounts and billing information;

- undertakings to be satisfied; and

- any other specific subfolders appropriate to the file.

Where possible, you should consider having an employee review client files periodically to ensure that their contents are organized efficiently and tidily, and that relevant dates are noted.

Regardless of the organization system that you choose to implement, for it to be effective you must ensure that it is followed.

PRESERVING CLIENT PROPERTY

Property is a very broad concept. It can be defined as anything that is owned by an identifiable person or group of persons. It includes homes, land, and vehicles, as well as intellectual property—that is, ideas and inventions under copyright or trademark.

Rule 3.07 deals with client property, and the obligation of paralegals to preserve such property when it is entrusted to them. The term **client property** covers a wide range of items, such as money or other valuables, physical items, and information (guideline 10); it includes retainer funds and any other funds or property given to you for safekeeping. Before accepting property to safeguard, you must satisfy yourself that you are able to keep it safe and that in doing so you will not inadvertently be participating in a crime—for example, by having stolen property or evidence in your possession. You may refuse to take client property into your possession if you have any concerns of this nature.

According to By-law 9, s. 18, paralegals should maintain a **valuable property record** in order to document storage and delivery of client property. This may include stocks, bonds, or other securities in bearer form; jewellery, fur, paintings, collector's items, or any saleable valuables; and any other property that a paralegal could possibly convert into cash (guideline 10). The valuable property record should not include items that cannot be sold or negotiated by the paralegal, such as wills, securities registered in the name of the client, corporate seals, or records. These items should be listed carefully, but separately from the valuable property record.

The valuable property record is an important tool for managing client property and may be useful should you need to defend yourself against complaints or claims made by clients.

client property
property owned by the client, including money or other valuables, physical items, and information (guideline 10), as well as retainer funds and any other funds or property given to a paralegal for safekeeping

valuable property record
a written record that documents the paralegal's receipt, storage, and delivery of all client property other than trust funds

STORING ACTIVE FILES

Your office procedures must allow you to protect client confidentiality in accordance with rules 3.03(1) and 3.03(3). Guideline 8 provides helpful advice regarding how to store active client files appropriately in order to ensure this.

First, you should physically position files in a way that is mindful of your confidentiality obligations. Client files must be kept out of sight. You should consider keeping filing cabinets in a discreet location away from the reception area and locking them when no one is in the office. Computer screens should be located and angled in such a way as to prevent people not in the firm (that is, non-employees) from viewing them, and you should consider using privacy screens for laptops. Finally, you should consider limiting access to particular client files to only those staff who are working on the matter, shredding confidential information before discarding it, and ensuring appropriate security for off-site storage of files.

You must also take appropriate steps to protect the confidentiality of client information in electronic form. This may include using firewall software, encrypting information, and using passwords where appropriate. If you are travelling with a laptop that contains client information, you should be particularly careful and should be advised that when crossing international borders your laptop may be subject to search and seizure or to a review of its files. Electronic data transfer over an encrypted communications channel—such as zipped files sent through email networks—may be a better means of transmitting client data.

CLOSING AND STORING INACTIVE CLIENT FILES

When matters to which a client file relates are completed or if the client terminates the retainer, you must close the client file. Closed files should be kept separate from active files. Closed client files should be assigned codes and stored in an orderly, retrievable manner in a single location. Closed paper files can be sent to a secure, off-site storage location, while closed electronic files should be retained in a manner that allows them to be searchable and accessible.

Because your duty of confidentiality to your clients lasts indefinitely—including after a client's death—you must ensure that you protect your clients' confidentiality after the files become inactive. Client files must be closed, and confidential materials disposed of, carefully. Simply throwing closed files into a dumpster without shredding them first, for example, would be a potential breach of your duty.

The process of closing files should involve, first of all, a review of the file. All unnecessary items should be removed, such as first drafts of pleadings or correspondence, and individual documents returned to the appropriate parties. Documents that a client gives to you in the course of your professional relationship remain the property of the client, and the client should be provided with all such documents. Generally, documents that belong to the client include:

- the client's original documents and photographs;

- originals or copies of documents prepared for the client;

- copies of documents for which the client has paid;

- the opposing party's documents;

- pleadings and court documents;

- expert reports; and

- copies of case law or legal memoranda, where the client has paid for the research.

Having the client sign an acknowledgment of receipt of the file contents upon closure of the file is good practice. In addition, when closing a file you should retain a copy of all documents returned to the client for your own records in the form of either paper copies or scanned documents. You will need these in the event that you are required to defend against a negligence claim or a complaint to the LSUC.

CONCLUSION

Unreserved communication between paralegals and their clients is essential for effective legal advice, and is facilitated by confidentiality. You should take steps to increase the likelihood that your communications with clients will be privileged, and you must avoid inadvertent disclosure of confidential information. Do not disclose confidential information about one client to another, or disclose having been consulted or retained by a particular person unless the nature of the matter requires it. Avoid indiscreet conversations about your clients' affairs, and do not partake in or repeat gossip related to a client's affairs.

Implement office procedures that allow you to protect client confidentiality and avoid conflicts of interest. Among other procedures, you might record identifying information and particulars about every client or potential client and use this to screen for conflicts of interest; establish a communication policy with each client; set up your office and storage systems to protect confidentiality; take steps to protect confidential information obtained and sent in electronic form; train and supervise all staff to ensure they understand their obligations with respect to confidentiality; and limit access to confidential information by outside service providers.

You should open a new client file every time a client retains your services, even if the file contains only the date and time of a consultation. The file should be opened only after a conflict check has been performed and no conflict has been found. You must document all work to be done and dates of importance regarding client files. Checklists and tickler systems can help you meet your obligations in this area; the latter can also help you manage other business-related obligations, such as payment of bills. You may use electronic or paper-based systems, and may choose to keep checklists and tickler systems for client service obligations, business management, and personal obligations separate or to combine them in a single system.

If you charge for your time, you must use a time docket to keep track of billable and non-billable time. Both are crucial to the operation of a successful, ethical, and financially viable practice. While you will seek to maximize your billable time, your ability to make appropriate use of non-billable time will greatly enhance your practice and your reputation in the long term.

To document storage and delivery of client property, you should maintain a valuable property record. If you have any concerns about the property a client is asking you to safeguard—such as that in accepting it you may be participating in a crime—you may refuse to take the property into your possession.

Employ a file organization system that allows you to store and efficiently retrieve information about clients and opposing parties; screen for conflicts; check for limitation periods; close, retain, and appropriately dispose of client files; review and make changes to management systems to keep them effective and up to date; identify and place clients' property in safekeeping; and comply with the LSUC's bookkeeping and record-keeping requirements.

To protect client confidentiality, client files must be kept out of sight. Consider keeping filing cabinets away from the reception area and locking them when no one is in the office, and limiting access to particular client files to only those staff who are working on the matter. Locate and angle computer screens so that non-employees cannot view them, and use privacy screens for laptops. Shred confidential information before discarding it, and ensure appropriate security for off-site storage of files.

When closing a file, return any documents that belong to the client to the client, and have the client sign an acknowledgment of receipt of the file contents. Keep scanned copies or photocopies of all documents in the file for your records. Store closed paper and electronic client files in an orderly, retrievable manner in a single location.

KEY TERMS

billable time

checklist

client property

non-billable time

tickler

time docket

valuable property record

USEFUL URLS

Farcht, John. "A Checklist for an Efficient Home Office Work Area." http://www.homeofficeweekly.com/office-space/efficient-work-area.html.

Law Technology News. http://www.lawtechnews.com/r5/home.asp.

Paralegal Today. "Litigation Checklist." http://www.legalassistanttoday.com/forms/2007/ma07/BTN%201.5%20Litigation%20Checklist.DOC.

Perman, Matt. 2009. "A Few Quick Examples on How to Make Your Tickler Electronic." http://www.whatsbestnext.com/2009/03/a-few-quick-examples-on-how-to-make-your-tickler-file-electronic.

REFERENCES

Collis, D., and C. Forget. *Working in a Legal Environment.* Toronto: Emond Montgomery, 2007.

Law Society of Upper Canada (LSUC). "By-Laws." 2005. http://www.lsuc.on.ca/regulation/a/by-laws.

Law Society of Upper Canada (LSUC). "Paralegal Professional Conduct Guidelines." Toronto: LSUC, 2008. http://www.lsuc.on.ca/paralegals/a/paralegal-professional-conduct-guidelines.

Law Society of Upper Canada (LSUC). "Paralegal Rules of Conduct." Toronto: LSUC, 2007, as amended. http://www.lsuc.on.ca/paralegals/a/paralegal-rules-of-conduct.

Law Society of Upper Canada (LSUC). "Practice Management Guidelines." Toronto: LSUC, 2009. http://rc.lsuc.on.ca/pdf/pmg/pmg.pdf.

REVIEW QUESTIONS

1. How can paralegals avoid inadvertent disclosure of confidential information?

2. What are some office procedures that paralegals can employ to prevent breaches of confidentiality?

3. What is a tickler system?

4. What is a checklist, and what functions does it serve?

5. What is a time docket, and why is it useful?

6. When deciding how to organize client files, what must paralegals ensure that their systems allow them to do?

7. What is a valuable property record, and what kinds of items should it include? What kinds of items should it not include?

8. What must a paralegal do when matters to which a client file relates are completed or when the client terminates the retainer?

9. Explain how inactive or closed client files should be stored.

Glossary

advertising   efforts to draw attention to a product or a business in order to encourage sales, generally through paid announcements in various media

asset   item of value owned by a company or person, including tangible items such as buildings and equipment, and intangible ones such as telephone numbers and licences

asset sale   a sale in which a business's tangible assets are sold, but not its name, corporate identity, and goodwill

billable time   time that is charged to a client

budget   a list of anticipated income and expenses for a defined future period

business communication   communication for the purpose of carrying out business activities; includes marketing, customer relations, branding, community engagement, advertising, public relations, and employee management

business plan   a document that contains a summary of a business's operational and financial objectives, along with detailed plans and budgets that explain how the objectives will be achieved

cash flow   movement of money into and out of a business

checklist   a list of things to be done or steps to be taken in relation to a file or other aspect of business management

client   a purchaser of services; includes, but is not limited to, a former client, and a client of the paralegal firm of which the paralegal is a partner or employee, whether or not the paralegal handles the client's work (rule 1.02)

client profile   data relating to the demographics of a business's potential clients—such as their geographic location, age, income level, gender, ethnicity, and education level—that allows business owners to assess the needs of their target market

client property   property owned by the client, including money or other valuables, physical items, and information (guideline 10), as well as retainer funds and any other funds or property given to a paralegal for safekeeping

competent paralegal   a paralegal who has and applies the relevant skills, attributes, and values appropriate to each matter undertaken on a client's behalf (rule 3.01(4))

confidential information   any information that paralegals gain in the course of their professional relationship with a client; paralegals have a duty to hold all such information in strict confidence indefinitely and may not disclose it to any other person, unless authorized to do so by the client or required to do so by law (rule 3.03(1))

conflict of interest   an interest, financial or otherwise, that may negatively affect a paralegal's ability to fulfill the professional and ethical obligations owed to a client

contingency fee   a fee paid based on a percentage of the final settlement or judgment, and therefore payable only if the client is successful

corporation   a business entity that has a legal existence separate and apart from that of the individuals who created it or who operate it

delegate   to assign tasks to others

due diligence   investigation of a business or a person, or the performance of an act to ensure compliance with legal or other standards

entrepreneur   an individual who starts up a new business

errors and omissions insurance   the insurance that covers an individual licensee in the event that a client is successful in suing for professional negligence; also called professional liability insurance

ethics   a branch of philosophy that seeks to address questions about morality; a codified set of moral rules specific to the performance of professional obligations

fiduciary duty   an obligation, with respect to financial matters, to put the interests of the person owed the duty above one's own interests

financial analysis   a comparison by a business of its budgeted numbers with actual ones to find explanations for differences between its anticipated and actual earnings and expenses, and to help it determine such things as whether it is setting appropriate fees, renting suitable office space, and so on

financial plan   a key component of a business plan that concerns the money coming into and going out of the business; shows how much money is required to operate the business and where that money is coming from

goodwill   an intangible asset consisting of a business's reputation, competitive advantage, and brand, measured by the fair market value of the business less its book value

joint and several liability   shared liability, such that all parties are equally liable for the full amount of the debt or obligation

Law Society of Upper Canada (LSUC)   a professional organization that governs legal services in Ontario with a mandate to ensure that the people of Ontario are served by lawyers and paralegals who meet set standards of education, competence, and conduct

legal services   services that involve applying legal principles and legal judgment to the circumstances and objectives of a client

liabilities   debts and other financial obligations

limited liability partnership   a partnership of professionals where not all of the partners are liable for the professional negligence of one or some of the partners

limited partnership   a type of partnership that restricts liability to only one or some of the partners, as set out in a partnership agreement

management plan   the part of a business plan that outlines how the business is structured and describes the responsibilities of various individuals with respect to its management

market analysis   used by business owners, in the planning stages of their business and on an ongoing basis, to help them determine the opportunities and risks of a particular market and how these may affect their success

market profile   a business tool, created through research, that provides business owners with important information about areas of opportunity in the market— for example, common legal problems in a particular market

marketing   a broader concept than advertising that focuses on branding, such as with use of letterhead, business cards, and logos (rule 8.03)

marketing plan   a document that sets out actions identified as necessary for a business to achieve its marketing objectives

multi-discipline partnership   a partnership of licensees and other professionals, such as accountants and tax consultants, through which paralegals can provide their clients with non-legal professional services that support the provision of legal services

non-billable time   time docketed but not billed to a client, such as time spent on professional development, continuing education, marketing, and business management

paralegal   an individual who provides legal services and representation in permitted practice areas, and who has a licence to do so issued by the LSUC

partnership   a form of business in which two or more persons carry on business together with a reasonable expectation of a profit; also called a general partnership

professional   a member of a vocation founded upon specialized education and training and subject to standards of competence and ethics

professional corporation   a corporation that protects shareholder-owners against personal liability but not against professional liability; must be authorized by the LSUC

professional responsibility   refers to paralegals' obligations to observe the rules and ethics of the paralegal profession as determined by the LSUC

retainer   the advance payment made by a client, usually at the time that the retainer agreement is signed, which is deposited in the paralegal's trust account

retainer agreement   a contract between the client and the paralegal that confirms that the paralegal has been hired to provide legal services to the client, and defines the parameters of the relationship

sole proprietorship   a business owned by a single individual, where there is no legal distinction between the owner of the business and the business itself

standard of care   the level of care, competence, or prudence required to avoid liability for negligence

strategic planning   the process of assessing the current business situation and the environment to determine whether it is changing, and revising the business plans to reflect the findings

tickler   a system that is used to provide notice of future obligations and events, such as court dates, meetings, limitation periods, and other deadlines

time docket   a record of time spent on billable and non-billable matters detailing work done, for how long, and on what matter

trust account   a separate account that paralegals must maintain to keep client funds held in trust

valuable property record   a written record that documents the paralegal's receipt, storage, and delivery of all client property other than trust funds

Index